The Labor Arbitration Guide

The Labor Arbitration Guide

WALTER E. BAER

 1974

DOW JONES-IRWIN, INC. Homewood, Illinois 60430

First Printing, May 1974

ISBN 0-87094-073-2

Library of Congress Catalog Card No. 73–91795

Printed in the United States of America

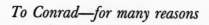

To Conrad—for many reasons

Preface

THERE ARE two types of labor arbitration. One is involved in writing the labor agreement, or contract, between a company and a union. The other is designed to interpret the contract and aid the parties in the administration of the agreements it contains. In the common vernacular of collective bargaining, the first is called "contract arbitration;" the second, "grievance arbitration." The two are sharply different. It is with the latter that this volume is concerned.

Grievance arbitration, which provides an alternative to strikes and lockouts, has been referred to as a judicial process because it requires the arbitrator to interpret that private source of law which regulates the parties, the labor agreement. As a dispute-settling process, it is almost as old as the recorded history of man—history relates how Solomon acted as the wise and respected neutral.

Approximately 94 percent of all labor-management agreements in this country provide for grievance arbitration for the peaceful resolution of disputes, and the use of such arbitration is growing. Each year more of the nation's workers are being organized by unions. Each year the number of existing labor agreements is increasing. Each year more and more cases are being referred to arbitration. Each year new arbitrators are entering the profession and struggling for acceptance and recognition. And each year, thousands of individuals find themselves assigned the responsibility of preparing for, and then presenting, a case before an arbitrator as advocates and representatives of their companies or unions.

It is to all of these current and potential practitioners in the mystical processes of arbitration that this volume is directed. If it serves in any way to remove any of the questions, doubts, or mysteries which surround the process or to enable any such advocates to function more ably—or more comfortably—it will have served its purpose.

April 1974   W. E. BAER

Contents

1

What Is Arbitration?

WHAT is meant by the arbitration of labor disputes? How did it originate? How does it work? What is its purpose? Does it in fact serve that purpose? These and a myriad of other questions trouble the minds of thousands of newcomers to the arbitration process each year and arise frequently in the minds of many who have been practitioners in the field for some time.

DEFINITIONS

Conceptions of "arbitration" vary. A management representative has said, "Arbitration is a means by which the Union is enabled to further erode management's few remaining prerogatives by obtaining things through a third party which were not given nor intended to be given during collective bargaining."

On the other hand, a union representative has called arbitration "the process which allows an outsider, who was not present when the parties argued, compromised and finally agreed, to come in and look over the shoulders of the Company and Union, to read their agreement, hear their respective arguments, then tell them what they *really* meant and intended when they drafted their document—and thus provide justice and equity to all."

1

Professor George W. Taylor has said, "In a very real sense, the parties who establish their own labor arbitration machinery create a judicial procedure where none has existed." (1)

Professor Harry Shulman, a statesman in the field of arbitration, has expanded that view:

> To consider . . . arbitration as a substitute for court litigation or as the consideration for a no-strike pledge is to take a foreshortened view of it. In a sense it is a substitute for both—but in the sense in which a transport plane is a substitute for a stagecoach. The arbitration is an integral part of the system of self-government. And the system is designed to aid management in its quest for efficiency, to assist union leadership in its participation in the enterprise, and to secure justice for the employees. It is a means of making collective bargaining work and thus preserving private enterprise in a free government. (2)

Another function of the arbitration process was dramatically described by Louis L. Jaffe, professor and arbitrator, as he discussed the dynamics of the arbitration hearing and the rôles of its participants:

> Arbitration . . . is a school, an arena, a theatre. Everyone both participates and observes. The whole company of actors—arbitrator, union and employer officials, the griever, and the witnesses (mostly employees)—sits at one table. Argument, assertion, testimony, charge and countercharge, even angry abuse—sometimes spontaneous, sometimes "for the record"—flow freely in quick, continuous intercourse. The arbitrator may let the discussion take its head for a moment, then rein it in, an occasional question, a request for clarification. Because the process is relatively free, it may assume many forms, some quiet and orderly, some volatile and discordant. The form is in fact a function of the general labor relation—of the maturity, the degree of mutual understanding and respect, the intelligence of the opposing officials. . . . Arbitration takes its stand in the very current of industrial life. The scene, the dramatis personae, the vocabulary, being familiar, raise no barriers to comprehension. The worker sees his case analyzed by his leaders, among whom I include the employer as well as union officials. They reveal the clashing propositions at the heart of the grievance. The arbitrator relates his answer to basic industrial premises. (3)

Arbitration, then, may be described as a substitute for litigation, a means for averting economic confrontations between the parties, and a procedure for obtaining a final and binding resolution in an otherwise unresolvable dispute. Arbitration includes all of these, as well as, perhaps, the purposes imputed by the management and union representatives quoted above. Perhaps, too, it is more than all of these things.

The arbitration process was established primarily as a peaceful means for resolving disputes between labor and management without either's having to resort to other forms of economic force.

Management's quest for stability and efficiency, ensured by the guarantee of continuity of operations, which took the form of a no-strike agreement from the employees and the union, left the union without its strongest weapon, the strike, to resolve its grievance disputes with management.

To achieve its objective of untroubled and uninterrupted operations, management was obliged to provide some equitable system for dispute resolution if it expected the union to sacrifice its primary power, the use of economic force. The grievance and arbitration provisions of the labor agreement were supposed to provide just such a fair, equitable, and just solution to the parties' problems during the term of the contract.

Arbitration has served these purposes well, in that the objective of securing some semblance of industrial peace has been realized. Before commending the virtues of arbitration, however, some recognition must be accorded its critics, for the process has certainly not been immune from criticism—much of it valid and at least some of it constructively intended.

Management representatives claim that the union uses the arbitral forum as an excuse for engaging in "fishing expeditions." Occasionally this does happen. A union may have failed to obtain some contract concession at the bargaining table. Later it may try to obtain that same concession, interpretation, or practice through the grievance and arbitration processes. There are occasions when such an unintended use of the arbitration system does indeed produce a supportive award.

There are even occasions when a union will seek to obtain through the arbitration processes some concession, interpretation, or practice that it had not sought or even mentioned throughout the many bargaining sessions that led ultimately to a consummated agreement. And at times this improper use of arbitral processes results in a concession to which the union is not entitled.

Such misuses of the system of labor arbitration clearly violate the purpose for which it was established. But it must be said that management is sometimes guilty of similar practices.

Too often employers themselves frustrate the union in its attempts to obtain equitable settlement of issues within the machinery of the grievance procedure. The wrongful denial of legitimate complaints sometimes leaves the union no choice but to press the matter into arbitration. Because the arbitral process is merely another creation of man and thus contains certain inevitable imperfections, arbitrators occasionally support management's position on issues that should not be upheld.

Whether management's position is wrongfully taken out of obstinacy, from a deliberate attempt to frustrate the union, a calculated intention to force the union to an otherwise avoidable expenditure of money, or because of a personality clash rather than because of an honest difference in contractual interpretation, the result is the same—the arbitral processes are unethically and improperly used.

The union representative's remarks cited in the beginning point to other inherent deficiencies of arbitration. It is true that the arbitrator selected to resolve a dispute has not been one of the parties present at the collective bargaining table. He has not been privy to all of the proposals and counterproposals exchanged and finally abandoned, all of the contentions and arguments, and all of the discussions about intended contractual interpretations. He does not know which issues argued before him were in fact never discussed between the parties during bargaining sessions. It goes without saying that an arbitrator cannot be as intimately informed of the realities and of the validity of the claims as the principals themselves. Like the hearing officer of a court of appeals, the labor arbitrator is dependent upon the honesty, integrity, articulateness, skill, and expertise of the advocates who appear before him.

However, in its defense, it should be pointed out that although the arbitration process has loopholes that allow for these and other misuses of the system, they arise not so much from the process as from the human failings of its practitioners. Despite infrequent misuses, the process continues to serve a useful purpose. If it were not for the availability of orderly and peaceful arbitral arrangements, the parties would have to resort to some other means—undoubtedly less orderly and less peaceful—for resolving their differences, no matter how improper or specious the issue.

Critics of arbitration point to still other shortcomings. Because each will be discussed at greater length in later chapters, they will only be touched upon briefly here. They say that the process is too slow. That it takes too long to select an arbitrator, too long to get the arbitrator to the hearing table, and too long after the close of the hearing for the arbitrator to render his award. All of this is often true, and occurs too frequently.

It is claimed that the process is too expensive, and that the costs vary too much from one arbitrator to another. The parties may hold a one-day hearing before a given arbitrator and receive a total bill of $500. They may hold another one-day hearing before a different arbitrator and be charged $1,000 or more. This only demonstrates that arbitrators are human, that some are more mercenary than others, or that some have a higher regard for their individual knowledge and professional worth than others. All of this is true and too frequently experienced.

It is claimed that some arbitrators "scoreboard"—that is, they premeditatedly and calculatingly fashion their decisions and awards so as to maintain themselves in good favor with both parties and preserve their continued acceptability to both. They allegedly do so by giving employers approximately one half of the favorable decisions and the union the other half. In this manner they presumably attempt to exhibit a public record that graphically demonstrates their impartiality. There may be some substance to this claim, but the incidence, I believe, is so relatively infrequent as to not be worthy of professional concern.

Another contention holds that certain arbitrators are pro-union or pro-management. Undoubtedly there are some with secretly held sentiments toward or against one side or the other. But the contention is that the rulings of some arbitrators consistently reflect such sentiments. There may be some small substance to this claim. But the careers of such arbitrators will be short-lived. Word will get around. The labor-management community has its own close-knit fraternity, which encourages the sharing of such information from employer to employer, union to union, consultant to client, and attorney to attorney.

There is no denying that the arbitration system is not without its risks—that the union sacrifices its right to strike in return for adjudication before a stranger who may not understand or sympathize with it, and that management surrenders its right to unilateral determination of what is right and wrong, on the basis of its more experienced viewpoint and its vested interests, to an outsider who has no responsibility for the conduct of the business. But the overwhelming weight of evidence serves primarily to give witness to the virtues of the arbitration process. As an institution, it is far from new. In fact, it existed for many centuries prior to the establishment of English common law. At least one court, the Kansas City Court of Appeals, has called arbitration "the oldest known method of settlement of disputes between men." (4) Solomon functioned as an arbitrator almost 3,000 years ago.

HISTORY

We are concerned here, however, with more recent history: briefly, the developments of the past 30 years and, more importantly, the current state and style of arbitration practice. In 1942, the National War Labor Board was created by executive order. The War Labor Disputes Act of 1943 gave it statutory authority. Beginning primarily at that time, a large number of today's oldest, most established arbitrators started to accumulate a wealth of arbitral experience. That experience and considerable exposure to dispute settlements since have provided many of today's most respected and sought-after arbitrators with envied reputations. The majority of the 20,000 disputes resolved during World War II were labor conflicts involving the provisions of collective bargaining agreements. The policies of the War Labor Board contributed substantially to the advancement of labor arbitration in American industry, inasmuch as they required the parties to formulate contractual provisions for arbitrating their future disputes, which involved applying and interpreting the labor agreement. (5) Today, the overwhelming majority of labor contracts provide for arbitration as the terminal point for disputes unresolved after processing through the grievance machinery.

The alternatives are few. The parties to labor disputes could resort to industrial warfare. They could strike, slow down, withhold production, withhold jobs, or engage in sit-downs, work stoppages, lockouts, and a myriad of other self-destructive practices. Or they could turn to the courts of law, which are ill equipped to cope with such matters and too far removed to have a sophisticated understanding of the peculiar problems faced by industrial parties.

The labor arbitration process may not be perfect, but it does work. To date, no one has devised a more viable alternative.

Federal policy has recognized that the grievance-arbitration procedure in collective bargaining is a major factor in achieving industrial peace.

The 1947 Labor Management Relations Act, section 201, reads:

> That it is the policy of the United States that—
>
> (a) Sound and stable industrial peace and the advancement of the general welfare, health and safety of the Nation and of the best interests of employer and employees can most satisfactorily be secured by the settlement of issues between employers and employees through the processes of conference and collective bargaining between employers and the representatives of their employees;
>
> (b) The settlement of issues between employers and employees through collective bargaining may be advanced by making available full and adequate governmental facilities for conciliation, mediation, and *voluntary arbitration* to aid and encourage employers and the representatives of their employees to reach and maintain agreements concerning rates of pay, hours, and working conditions, and to make all reasonable efforts to settle their differences by mutual agreement reached through conferences and collective bargaining or by such methods as may be provided for in any applicable agreement for the settlement of disputes. (Italics added.)

The relevant portion of the act goes on to state in section 202:

> (a) There is hereby created an independent agency to be known as the Federal Mediation and Conciliation Service.

The Federal Mediation and Conciliation Service (FMCS)

The Federal Mediation and Conciliation Service (FMCS), thus mandated by law to advance free collective bargaining as a means of attaining labor-management accord in the United States, considered its arbitration services an integral part of its efforts to fulfill that responsibility.

Over the years, the general counsel of the service has responded to continuously mounting requests for qualified arbitrators through the development of improved methods and an expanding staff.

The continuing expansion of private-sector arbitration requirements, the prospect of whole new sectors of the labor market becoming users of arbitration services, and the need for the further development of labor arbitration itself provide some of the dimensions of the service's task. (How the service is meeting these new arbitral demands is discussed later in this chapter.)

The FMCS is the principal government agency with responsibilities in the field of labor arbitration. Under its policies and procedures, the service assists the parties in labor-management disputes by nominating independent arbitrators qualified to hear cases at issue. The regulations of the service govern those arbitration cases that arise between parties who have contractually agreed to utilize the FMCS arbitration services for the settlement of grievance disputes during the life of their agreement. Once an arbitrator has been selected by the parties from nominees provided by the office of the general counsel, the service withdraws from active participation in the case in recognition of the private nature of the relationship between the parties and their chosen arbitrators. However, the service does retain an interest in the case to ensure that it is processed promptly and that it proceeds in accordance with the regulations of the service.

The chart below indicates the arbitration-unit workload of the FMCS in three representative years selected for comparison purposes.

	1971	1967	1961
Requests for panels or direct appointments......................	12,327	6,955	3,174
Panels submitted......................	13,235	7,623	3,347

In the 11 fiscal years between 1961 and 1971, the requests for panels or appointments increased by almost 400 percent. In the same period, the number of panels submitted also expanded by almost 400 percent. The requests for panels reached an annual record level in 1971 with the figure of 12,327 requests, representing a jump of 22.8 percent over the previous fiscal year. The service-provided panels in 1971 constituted an increase of 18.9 percent over those of the 1970 fiscal year. In addition, it must be remembered that each submitted panel of arbitrators consisted, on an average, of seven names.

In response to the growing demands of the parties, the FMCS arbitration services were reorganized in 1972. Under the development program, a computerized data-processing system was created, the administrative and monitoring procedures were revised, and the scope of attention given arbitration matters by the agency was expanded.

The name of the computerized arbitration-information system, ARBIT, was formed from the first letters of the larger descriptive title, the FMCS Arbitrator Information Tracking System. A modification of an information-retrieval system developed by the National Aeronautics and Space Administration (NASA), the ARBIT system is capable of maintaining and producing data necessary for rapid and accurate arbitrator-panel selection, with a virtually unlimited capacity for record storage and the ability to select information from those records almost simultaneously.

Upon receipt of a request for a panel of arbitrators, ARBIT can supply the names of all the arbitrators on the roster who practice in or near the place where the arbitration is to be held, and who meet other specific criteria requested by the parties. The FMCS is able to respond to specific requests in special cases for arbitrators with specific experience or skills.

Once the panel is selected from the names generated, the records maintained by the computer are automatically posted and letters are produced by high-speed printers notifying the parties of the arbitrators nominated for their case. The ARBIT system maintains up-to-date information on the status of cases by case number, arbitrator's personal file, company file, and union file. Subsequent activity in the case is monitored, posted, and followed up as it progresses through the appointment of an arbitrator, the hearing of the case, and the filing of an award to close the case. Through the use of automatic time thresholds established for each case, ARBIT monitors the progress of each case and notifies the general counsel of FMCS when delays at any stage are imminent.

A special feature incorporated into the system is the automatic production of current biographical sketches, which accompany the names of the panel members sent to the parties. Such current information is important both to those selecting arbitrators and to the arbitrators themselves, since it will ensure more accurate evaluation and selection, on the one hand, and improved presentation, on the other. This feature is especially important to new arbitrators seeking increased acceptability, since their biographical

TABLE 1–1

Issues for which FMCS Provided Arbitration Services, Fiscal Year 1971

General

New or reopened contract terms	33
Contract interpretation or application	2,150

Issues

Discharge and disciplinary actions	1,009
Incentive rates or standards	63
Job evaluation	344
Promotion and upgrading	169
Layoff, bumping and recall	208
Transfer	73
Other seniority issues	92
Overtime pay	151
Overtime distribution	178
Compulsory overtime	18
Union officers—superseniority and union business	23
Strike or lockout issues	18
Vacations and vacation pay	99
Holidays and holiday pay	85
Scheduling of work	147
Reporting, call-in, and call-back pay	51
Health and welfare	34
Pensions	7
Other fringe benefits	65
Subcontracting	66
Jurisdictional disputes	31
Foreman, supervision, etc.	54
Mergers, consolidations, accretion, other plants	5
Working conditions, including safety	31
Miscellaneous	209

sketches will immediately reflect each increment of experience gained.

In addition to improving the quality and efficiency of FMCS arbitration services, ARBIT is intended to ensure a more equitable distribution of cases among available arbitrators. Through the automatic display of current case nominations, appointments, and awards with each arbitrator's name, the system will be able to choose arbitrators available for prompt hearings, avoiding thereby the repeated use of arbitrators already burdened with case backlogs. Similarly, information on arbitrators currently unavailable, special requirements of parties, and other notes are displayed in the system.

In addition to the advantages of speed and flexibility, the FMCS gains through ARBIT a means of increased control and a diagnostic tool. Because the FMCS is concerned about increasing delays and mounting costs of arbitration, ARBIT is intended to monitor arbitration activity conducted under its auspices and identify areas of special needs and problems, sources of delays, and inconsistent cost patterns. Since all FMCS arbitration cases will be administered through the use of this one facility, appropriate information will be available to its general counsel for appropriate action. In individual situations, follow-ups and assistance provided by the service may be all that is required to help the parties use the arbitration process to maximum advantage.

Table 1–1 illustrates the issues for which FMCS has provided arbitration service.

Table 1–2 gives sample results of duration and cost data in FMCS-arranged arbitration.

The reorganization of FMCS arbitration services was primarily

TABLE 1–2

Sample Results of Duration and Cost Data in FMCS-arranged Arbitration, Fiscal Years 1969–71

	Per Case Average		
	1969 (N = 643)	1970 (N = 722)	1971 (N = 719)
Hearing time charged (days).......	0.95	0.92	0.92
Travel time charged (days)........	0.38	0.35	0.39
Study time charged (days).........	1.70	1.66	1.65
Total time charged (days).........	3.03	2.93	2.96
Average per diem rate............	$145.09	$156.83	$163.88
Average fee charged..............	$432.03	$457.97	$480.88
Average expenses charged.........	$ 76.03	$ 81.91	$ 85.71
Average total charged.............	$511.06	$539.88	$566.59
Time between grievance filed and request for panel (days).........	77.6	81.4	83.3
Time between request date and list sent (days)....................	9.2	7.8	11.1
Time between date list sent and appointment (days).............	39.9	44.3	46.0
Time between appointment and hearing (days).................	63.7	63.1	63.4
Time between hearing and award (days).......................	50.3	49.0	47.7
Total time between request and award (days).................	163.1	164.2	168.2

motivated by the increasing volume of requests and the difficulties attendant upon that growth. However, it also contained other very important objectives, which included the following:

- To improve arbitration selection and administrative procedures to expedite responses to requests from the parties and to meet a maximum response time of one working day.
- To create a flexible system which will absorb anticipated increases in arbitration requests, while maintaining the new time standards. Increases are anticipated from growth of activity in both private and public sectors of industrial relations.
- To distribute cases equitably among available arbitrators.
- To develop the capability of responding to requests specifying more refined arbitrator experience criteria.
- To identify national arbitration requirements for the development of new arbitrator resources.
- To determine substantive trends in ad hoc arbitration through research for policy and program purposes.

In 1970 the Bureau of National Affairs, Inc. (BNA) published information that provides an up-to-date analysis of the widespread use of the arbitration process and its importance in collective bargaining documents. (6)

About 94 percent of all labor contracts provide for arbitration of grievances not settled by the parties. Such provisions appear in 95 percent of the manufacturing and 97 percent of the non-manufacturing contracts. It is interesting that in only three industries fewer than 90 percent of the contracts have arbitration clauses: construction (79 percent), primary metals (76 percent), and lumber (57 percent).

More than three fourths of all agreements provide for ad hoc

TABLE 1-3

Arbitration Procedures I(6) (frequency expressed as percentage of contracts)

	Provision for Arbitration	Type of Arbitration				
		Ad hoc	Permanent	Individual	Board	Individual of Board
Overall frequency............	94	77	18	56	41	4
Manufacturing...............	95	77	18	68	32	4
Nonmanufacturing...........	97	78	17	30	65	3

TABLE 1-4

Arbitration Procedure II (frequency expressed as percentage of contracts)

	Arbitral Agency			Choice of Arbiter	
	FMCS	AAA	Other	By Designation	By Selection from List
Overall frequency..............	33	26	13	25	51
Manufacturing................	35	31	8	22	52
Nonmanufacturing.............	29	23	22	31	41

selection of an arbitrator on a case-by-case basis. In 12 percent of the contracts, a single arbitrator is designated to hear all of the cases that arise during the term of the agreement. The remaining arrangements provide for establishment of a permanent board, designation of several umpires to serve on a rotation basis, and ad hoc selection from a list of arbitrators included in the contract.

The Arbitrators

The impartial agency called upon to assist in making the arbitrator selection is most often FMCS or the American Arbitration Association (AAA). A small portion of agreements designate assistance from some other source, such as a state mediation agency or a federal or state judge. With some overlapping, FMCS is appointed in approximately one third of the contracts; the AAA, in about 26 percent; and a small number of other agencies, in 13 percent. Interestingly, one fourth of labor agreements allow the impartial agency itself to appoint an arbitrator, while about 50 percent state that the agency will merely be asked to provide a list of names, from which the parties will make their own selection.

A majority of agreements (about 90 percent of all arbitration provisions) require the parties to turn to an impartial agency should the selection process reach an impasse.

Both FMCS and AAA much prefer to provide a panel of names and let the parties take it from there; only when the parties are adamant—less than 3 percent of the cases handled by FMCS—will the agencies make the selection. (6)

Contracts of larger companies tend to provide for a permanent arbitrator (or board of arbitrators), which the parties select and retain as long as the arrangement is mutually acceptable. In a few instances, the contract may also specify the selection of special arbitrators, by agreement of the parties, for grievances that do not fall under the general arbitration procedure.

In spite of the rapidly increasing demand for arbitrators, the average age of the really qualified arbiters in the United States is about 60 years. The majority of these men received their initial arbitration experience on government labor boards during World War II and/or the Korean War.

As Robert Coulson aptly noted, parties engaged in the "crystal-ball" selection of arbitrators "believe that their experience and judgment makes it possible for them to match the issue to the arbitrators much like the fisherman tempts the rainbow trout with

TABLE 1-5

Number of Cases Awarded per Labor Arbitration, AAA, 1970

	1	2-5	6-10	11-20	21-30	31
Number of cases awarded................	1	2-5	6-10	11-20	21-30	31
Number of arbitrators...................	142	149	69	50	24	24

the proper lure. . . . One by-product of all this expertise is that practitioners become hesitant to accept an unknown quality." (7)

The extent of this hesitancy is reflected in the AAA statistics. It was reported that in 1964, of 1,400 arbitrators on the association's national panel, only 370 actually rendered awards, while in 1970, 458 of 1,475 gave awards. Table 1-5 shows the uneven distribution of cases for 1970 among the 458 arbitrators, which further reveals the difficulty of achieving acceptance. (8)

Uneven distribution of cases is, of course, one of the factors that contributes to the problems of expense and delay. In their efforts to become established, newer arbitrators generally charge less. They are also typically more readily available than their busier professional associates.

A 1972 survey of 50 comparative newcomers who have become moderately active arbitrators on the panels of AAA since 1960 reveals the following:

• Their ages in 1972 ranged from 34 to 65.
• Their years on the AAA panel of active service ranged from 3 to 11 years.

- Ten had been employees of the National Labor Relations Board.
- Seventeen were previously employed by other federal agencies, including 3 with the War Labor Board and Wage Stabilization Board.
- Ten had been employees of city or state agencies.
- Twenty-five had been employed by management or labor or both.
- Two were alumni of the AAA.
- Seven of the fifty, the most active, had had experience as salaried assistants to well-known impartial chairmen.
- In respect to education, 31 had legal training, 27 had degrees in the social sciences, and 3 had industrial engineering degrees.
- The actual breakdown on current occupations was as follows: 15 lawyers, 21 educators, 12 full-time arbitrators, 1 industrial engineer, and 1 judge.
- Of the 12 self-styled full-time arbitrators: 4 had worked as assistants to impartial chairmen; 1 was a union official who, over 20 years ago, had been with the NLRB; 3 were from the New York State Mediation Board; 1 had recently retired from the NLRB; 1 recently had retired from the Massachusetts State Board; 1 had been a corporation executive for many years; 1 was a former FMCS official who had been labor counsel for a large industry for many years; and 6 of the 12 full-time arbitrators were lawyers.

This, then, is a representative listing of relatively new and untried, but otherwise qualified, apprentice arbiters. In the vast majority of cases, however, although they are new to the business of rendering impartial arbitral judgments, these newcomers have had extensive experience in, and exposure to, the arbitration process.

Some other interesting statistics bear on this particular matter. While the average age of members of the National Academy of Arbitrators was 49.7 years in 1952, in 1969 that average age had reached almost 60 years.

Table 1–6, showing the age distribution of academy members, bears some examination. The group is growing older and the percentage of the older group has doubled. The under-40 group has all but disappeared.

In the arbitration field, as I have pointed out, FMCS and AAA

TABLE 1–6

Age Distribution of Members of the National Academy of Arbitrators, by Year

Age	Percentage		
	1952	1962	1969
Under 40.....................	11.6	4.7	1.8
40–59........................	72.3	74.7	56.3
60 and over..................	16.1	20.7	41.9

serve as intermediaries between labor and management disputants. Since these agencies are in a position to give business and consequent financial rewards to private citizens, they must be very careful that, in the selection of persons for their roster and the nomination of these to the parties, they in no way discriminate among them or incur the charge that they have selected certain arbitrators for a favored role in the field. It has never been suggested that they are guilty of any such favoritism.

The National Academy of Arbitrators

Since this organization has been mentioned, perhaps it is in order to explain the role of the National Academy of Arbitrators. This can best be accomplished by citing an extract from its constitution:

Article II, Section 1—The Purposes for which the Academy is formed are: To establish and foster the highest standards of integrity, competence, honor, and character among those engaged in the arbitration of industrial disputes on a professional basis; to secure the acceptance of an adherence to the Code of Ethics for Arbitrators in labor-management Arbitration (being Part I of the Code of Ethics and Procedural Standards for Labor-Management Arbitration prepared by the American Arbitration Association and the National Academy of Arbitrators and approved by the Federal Mediation and Conciliation Service); to promote the study and understanding of the arbitration of industrial disputes; to encourage friendly association among the members of the profession; to cooperate with other organizations, institutions and learned societies interested in industrial relations, and to do any and all things which shall be appropriate in the furtherance of these purposes. [As amended January 27, 1965]

The National Academy of Arbitrators was founded at Chicago on September 14, 1947. In 1972 the membership roster totaled approximately 375.

The academy is not an agency for the selection or appointment of arbitrators. It initiates and sponsors activities designed to improve general understanding of the nature of arbitration and its use as a means of settling labor disputes. It meets annually in a national convention and more frequently in regional groupings. From time to time, the meetings are open to nonmembers.

In addition to its executive committee, the academy maintains standing committees on ethics and Grievance, Law and Legislation, and Membership. The "Code of Ethics and Procedural Standards," jointly promulgated by the academy and AAA, is the subject of continuing study and interpretative opinions by the ethics committee.

The academy reprints for its members lectures delivered at its meetings on various aspects of arbitration and it publishes yearly a volume containing the proceedings of its annual meetings. (9)

Membership in the National Academy of Arbitrators is conferred by vote of the board of governors upon recommendation of the membership committee of the academy. In considering applications for membership, the academy applies the following standards: (1) The applicant should be of good moral character, as demonstrated by adherence to sound ethical standards in professional activities. (2) The applicant should have substantial and current experience as an impartial arbitrator of labor-management disputes, or, alternatively, (3) the applicant with limited but current experience should have attained general recognition through scholarly publication or other activities as an impartial authority on labor-management relations. In evaluating the applicant's experience, the academy takes into account his general acceptability to the parties.

Membership is not conferred upon applicants primarily identified as advocates or consultants for labor or management in labor-management relations. The academy recognizes, nevertheless, that because of the fluid nature of the industrial relations field and the varied backgrounds and interests of its members, the relation of individual members to the field and their availability as arbitrators may change from time to time. Some members may be called upon to serve as consultants to private or public organizations;

some may act as advisors or advocates for labor or management; some may accept public office; some may act in still other capacities that render them for the time being unavailable for service as arbitrators. The academy does not consider that participation in such activities is necessarily inconsistent with continuous membership.

It should be noted that this organization aspires to the highest standards of professional ethics. Because of the professional standards required for membership in the academy, and hence the caliber of the arbiters among its ranks, a great number of labor-relations practitioners from both labor and management seek out academy members when making arbitral selections.

Of course, the rosters of the AAA and FMCS arbitration panels include a large number of members of the National Academy.

The Growing Scope of Arbitration

A few labor contracts make all grievance disputes eligible for arbitration, but, more often, certain specific matters are excluded. Among these items most frequently barred from arbitration are adjustments of production standards and administration of benefit plans.

The scope of arbitration was broadened in practice by the 1960 decisions of the U.S. Supreme Court in three cases commonly referred to as the "Steelworkers Trilogy." In these decisions, the Supreme Court largely limited the role of the courts in collective bargaining arbitration cases to determining whether (*a*) the claim of one of the parties was governed by the contract (not whether it had merit), (*b*) the contractual arbitration clause covered the dispute (if the dispute is *not clearly excluded* from arbitration, the courts should send the case to the arbitrator), and (*c*) the arbitrator based his award on the contract and remained within his authority (if he has done so, a court may not overrule him even though it disagrees with his award).

Representative of a *general* clause on the scope of arbitration is the following:

> Any dispute arising under the terms of this Agreement which cannot be settled between the parties involved may be submitted by either party on written notice to the other party, to an arbitration committee for their determination. (11)

Representative of a contract clause that makes specific items subject to arbitration is the following:

> Any controversy which has not been satisfactorily adjusted under the Grievance Procedure and which involves (A) the discharge of an employee or (B) the interpretation of provisions of this contract, or (C) an alleged violation of the contract may be submitted for settlement to the arbitration committee. (12)

Representative of a contract clause specifying that certain matters shall be *outside* the scope of arbitration is the following:

> Shift assignments are made by the company in accordance with production requirements. Both the Company and the Union recognize that some employees . . . may desire transfer to another shift . . . the shift change shall be made as openings permit and, where possible, in the order that the requests are received by the department. Grievances filed under this section of the Agreement shall be subject to the Grievance Procedure up to but not including Step 4, Arbitration. (13)

Clearly, contractual provision is concerned solely with the matter of shift transfers and with excluding such issues from the arbitration process.

A final example of a contractual clause dealing with the scope of arbitration is that of the Collins Radio Company and the Electrical Workers (IUE), which expires in April 1974:

> Arbitration under this Agreement shall be limited to the interpretation or application of the provisions of this agreement and to grievances that have been properly and timely processed through the grievance procedure, but shall exclude any alleged understanding, practice or other matter outside the terms of this Agreement.

Here, a number of items are precluded from a proper arbitration hearing, and, of course, arbitral authority is barred from deciding these matters on their merits.

Another matter which must be explored is the question of who has access to the arbitration process. In the final analysis, it is the contractual language that determines who may invoke the process. Contracts that permit the initiation of arbitration at the request of either party are most common, but some contracts provide that initiation can be made at the request of the union, by mutual agreement, or at the request of an individual employee or group of employees.

Representative of a clause that allows the individual employee access to the arbitration process is the following:

> A grievance dispute which was not resolved at the level of the Superintendent of Schools under the grievance procedure may be submitted by the aggrieved employee or . . . by the Chapter, to an arbitrator for decision if it involves the application or interpretation of this Agreement. (14)

The courts have held in a number of decisions that the grievance proviso of Section 9 (*a*) of the Labor Management Relations Act does not give employees the right to compel an employer to arbitrate their grievances under arbitration clauses of a collective-bargaining contract where the right to arbitrate is restricted to the union and the employer. The proviso does no more than to assure the employee's right to present his grievance directly to his employer to see if it can be settled. (15)

An example of an agreement that clearly excludes the individual employee from the right to initiate arbitration is the following:

> In the case of any grievance, question or dispute remaining unsettled at the conclusion of discussions under sub-paragraph four (4) above, the Union or the Company, but not an individual employee, may take to arbitration any matter including job classification or newly created or changed jobs, provided that the dispute to be arbitrated concerns the application or interpretation of this Agreement, either as to meaning of its terms or as to the rights of either party under those terms. (16)

This provision is explicit in its exclusion; however, the exclusion may be accomplished merely by omitting to mention the employee's right to invoke arbitral processes. An example follows:

> If the grievance is not settled in Step 3, the Union may appeal it, by giving written notice of such appeal to the Company, within ten (10) working days after receipt of the written answer of the Personnel Manager and/or his designated representative, to Arbitration in accordance with the procedure and conditions set forth in the Arbitration provisions of this Agreement. (17)

Such a provision would make it impossible for an individual employee to demand that the employer arbitrate his grievance when his union has declined to do so. If he has been inadequately or unfairly represented by the union in the processing of a grievance, the employee may have a remedy against the union, but he may not compel arbitration under a contract that does not expressly provide for such action. (18)

As mentioned previously, the arbitral process also may be opened, under certain contractual terms, only on mutual agreement of the parties. For example:

> In the event that a grievance cannot be satisfactorily settled in the foregoing steps, either the Company or the Union, with the consent and approval of the other first obtained, may declare the matter a subject for arbitration by an impartial arbitrator. (19)

This provision is not found often; the most common provision would be minus the words "with the consent and approval of the other first obtained." Without that phrase, the clause would enable either party to request arbitration of the other, and arbitration would not be conditional upon the other's consent.

Later in this volume, other contractual provisions and conditions relevant to initiation of the arbitral process will be examined.

In closing this chapter, it should be said that, in large measure, the cause of industrial peace has been served by the adoption of voluntary arbitration—which has enabled the parties to work together, unthreatened and uncoerced, to create a means of achieving agreement on their conflicting rights and interests. Arbitration may sometimes be slower than the parties desire, it may sometimes be more expensive than they want; it may sometimes produce results they question. However, when the alternatives to this peaceful process are considered, it is not always—or even frequently—too slow, too costly, or of too questionable an outcome. As countless practitioners in the labor-relations arena have remarked on countless occasions, "it may not be the best system ever devised by men, but no one has yet come up with a better one."

2

Selecting the Arbitrator

A GRIEVANCE has been processed through the contractual dispute-resolution machinery. The parties have met and discussed the issue in the progressive steps stipulated in the contract. The respective levels of management have met with the various officers of the union hierarchy. Viewpoints have been exchanged; arguments have been proferred and, it is hoped, weighed and considered by each party. The bargaining history has been explored; witnesses and principals in the dispute have been heard; relevant records examined; and pertinent contract language scrutinized and interpreted.

But the parties are unable to reach a mutually satisfactory settlement of their disagreement.

The matter is now being moved toward its last step, an arbitration hearing. What happens next?

First of all, let us examine the mechanics—that is, the instrument or means by which the issue is led into this final and binding process.

CONTRACTUAL PROVISIONS

A review of typical contractual arbitration provisions will illustrate how some parties have made prearbitration arrangements:

Arbitration—If the grievance shall not be satisfactorily adjusted through the above steps, the matter may proceed to arbitration, providing the Union notifies the Company of its desire to arbitrate and names its arbitrator within three (3) working days after the date of the regular Union meeting following the Production Manager's reply in Step Three. If the Union fails to notify the Company of its desire to arbitrate within the time stated, the grievance shall be considered dropped.

If the grievance is carried to arbitration as set forth above, the Company shall designate its arbitrator within five (5) working days or the grievance shall be considered granted.

If the two arbitrators named in the manner set forth above fail to agree on a third arbitrator within fifteen (15) days of the Company's designation, either party may request the Director of the Federal Mediation and Conciliation Service to appoint a panel of five (5) impartial, disinterested members. Each party shall have the right to challenge two members of the panel. The remaining member of the panel shall act as the Chairman of the Arbitration Committee. The written decision of the majority of arbitrators shall be final and binding upon both parties. The expenses and compensation incident to the service of the third arbitrator shall be determined in advance and paid jointly by the Company and Union. (20)

A brief analysis of this provision may provide helpful insights. First, in the initial paragraph, the time within which the union shall notify the company of its intent to arbitrate appears to be a fluctuating period, dependent upon how close the date of the union's next regular scheduled meeting is to the third and last grievance step. Further, at one point, the provision requires that the union shall "name its arbitrator" and, at another, that the company shall "designate its arbitrator." Presumably, this sets the structure for a tripartite arbitration forum. Actually, as the process evolves and functions, the union and company-appointed "arbitrators" operate as advocates for their respective parties and are certainly not impartial in the sense of being truly neutral third parties.

In the second paragraph, the language provides for the two appointed arbitrators (union and company advocates) to attempt to mutually agree on an informed, neutral third party, a bona fide arbitrator. Failure to agree is anticipated, in which case the selection process is to devolve on the Federal Mediation and Conciliation Service (FMCS). Interestingly, the wording could present potential problems to the parties. It does not appear to be incumbent on a given party to accept the obligation and responsibility of making a request to FMCS. Problems could result if neither moved to do so. Problems could result if each argued that it was the obligation of the other. Also, there does not appear to be a stipulated time period within which a party (which one?) is required to forward a panel request to FMCS. Problems could result if panel requests were long delayed—particularly if one party alleged that the delay of the other was undue and thereby raised a threshold issue of arbitrability, based on the claim of untimeliness of the request, causing alleged procedural defectiveness.

Still another point is that the second paragraph of this provision does not clearly spell out how the parties shall remove names from the FMCS-submitted panel. It merely says that "each party shall have the right to challenge two members of the panel." It does not stipulate that the parties shall alternately, and in turn, remove a name until only one of the initial five remains. It could be inferred that a party could remove any two names it wished, simultaneously. In any case, the contract does not indicate which party shall be first to remove a name or names, before the other party is afforded such opportunity. Nor does it provide a means, such as a coin flip, etc., for determining which party shall scratch the first name or names.

To suggest that any of the foregoing is nit-picking or tilting at windmills is not to face industrial realities. These have been real problems on numerous occasions. The labor-arbitration-research volumes contain hundreds of cases of this type.

One last point before leaving this provision: Its conclusion provides that the parties determine in advance the expenses of the arbitrator, which could be interpreted to mean that he should be paid in advance. Nevertheless, this requirement to determine full arbitral costs prior to a hearing is a rather unusual arrangement and often could be difficult if strictly adhered to.

Let us now look into another contractual provision, which is more explicit about the movement of grievances into arbitration and the selection of an arbitrator.

> Step 4. Arbitration. If no settlement is reached in Step 3 within the specified or agreed time limits, then either party may in writing, within ten work days thereafter, request that the matter be submitted to an arbiter for a prompt hearing as hereinafter provided in 19.6 to 19.9, inclusive.

Section 19.6.   Selection of Arbiter—By Agreement. In regard to each case reaching Step 4, the parties will attempt to agree on an arbiter to hear and decide the particular case. If the parties are unable to agree on an arbiter within ten work days after submission of the written request for arbitration, the provisions of 19.7 (Selection of Arbiter—From Arbitration Panel) shall apply to the selection of an arbiter.

Section 19.7.   Selection of Arbiter—From Arbitration Panel. Immediately following execution of this Agreement the parties will proceed to compile a list and agree upon a Corporate Panel of five arbiters. If a case reaches Step 4, and the parties are unable to agree to an arbiter within the time limit specified in 19.6, the case, irrespective of location, shall be heard and settled by an arbiter on the Corporate Panel if available. Assignment of cases to arbiters on the Corporate Panel shall be rotated in the alphabetical order of the last names of those available. An available arbiter is one who is available to conduct a hearing within sixty days (unless mutually extended) after expiration of the time limit specified in 19.6.

Section 19.8.   Procedure where Corporate Panel Not Available. In the event, as to any case, that there is no available arbiter on the Corporate Panel, the parties shall jointly request the American Arbitration Association to submit a panel of seven arbiters. Such request shall state the general nature of the case and ask that the nominees be qualified to handle the type of case involved. When notification of the names of the panel of seven arbiters is received, the parties in turn shall have the right to strike a name from the panel until only one name remains. The remaining person shall be the arbiter. The right to strike the first name from the panel shall be determined by lot. (21)

The draftsmanship of this provision is clearly superior. The language is neither vague nor uncertain in outlining the overall procedures to be followed. However, even this excellently written contract clause presents one potential problem to the parties—that is, presuming they do not already have an established practice or understanding. The last sentence reads: "The right to strike the first name from the panel shall be determined by lot."

First of all, what is "lot"? Presumably, in the context of this agreement, as in countless numbers of labor contracts, the term refers to some type of drawing or other determination chance.

But what type of determination? What form does it take? What if one party perceives this term to mean one kind of game or contest of chance, while the other considers it to be something quite different? What if each is stubborn or irresponsible—or what if only one party is either of these? What if one of the parties merely wishes to be disagreeable in order to prevent or frustrate the orderly processing of the claim to arbitration?

Vagueness in the terms of the contract may be a source of disagreement between two parties. But, that is not the extent of the problem presented by the above-quoted contractual language; it can be even more complicated, as it has been for various other parties.

To repeat, the sentence in question reads: "The right to strike the first name from the panel shall be determined by lot."

Let us assume that the parties can agree on the game of chance they will engage in. Let us assume that they draw straws from a vessel containing straws of various lengths, with the understanding that the one who draws the longer straw is considered the winner. Let us assume further that the company representative draws the longer straw. Who strikes the first name from the list of arbiters lying between the parties? The implication of the contractual language is that the winning party shall strike the first name. However, that is merely an inference; a reasonable man might interpret it to mean that the winning party then chooses which party is to strike the first name.

But why all this fuss about which party strikes the first name? Why is it significant, or even relevant?

The answer is that many labor-relations practitioners, representing either labor or management, consider that the party that does not strike the first name from an odd-numbered list of arbitrators is at an *advantage* when the list is ultimately reduced to only two names. A graphic example follows:

Arbitrator A—Company strikes
Arbitrator B—Union strikes
Arbitrator C—Company strikes
Arbitrator D—
Arbitrator E—

This is a simple example of five names. The company has struck the first name, A in the example; the union has struck arbitrator B; and the company has again struck, this time arbitrator C. It is now the union's turn, when only two names remain. By virtue of not having struck first, the union has the final choice between the two remaining names.

To some, this may seem a small matter; but, to many, it is a matter of great importance. In addition, the bigger the issue to be decided, the more critical the arbitral selection to the parties, and the greater the potential for dispute between them over who strikes the first name.

The potential for problems to arise because of vague terminology becomes more discernible when viewed in the light of the above example, and many have been the parties who have argued over such an issue. Many problems may be avoided by the use of precise contractual language.

In the following example, the provision specifies the party to go first:

> The parties shall first attempt to agree upon an impartial arbitrator. If they cannot agree within five (5) working days the parties shall jointly request the Federal Mediation and Conciliation Service to submit a list of five (5) names of possible arbitrators. First the Union, then the Company, shall alternately strike names from the list until only one (1) remains, and this person shall act as the arbitrator. (22)

Apparently these two parties resolved the question of which one was to strike the first name on the arbitral list during the course of their collective bargaining. In any case, it is a settled issue, and the union always strikes the first name.

Sometimes it is not specified which party is to strike first on each and every instance of arbitral selection. Nevertheless, the contractual provision may enable the parties to reach such determination. One such example follows:

> 7.02. If the parties cannot agree upon the selection of the Arbitrator, then the Party demanding arbitration shall, within five working days following the above-mentioned meeting, upon written notice to the other, request the Federal Mediation and Conciliation Service (address, office of General Counsel, Dept. of Labor Building, Fourteenth Street and Constitution Avenue, NW, Washington, D.C. 20427) to submit a list of seven (7) qualified arbitrators. All arbitrators listed must be currently a member of National Academy of Arbitrators.

> 7.03. Within three (3) working days of receipt of said list, the Parties will meet, and alternately and in turn strike a name until each Party has eliminated a total of three (3) names from the list. The Parties shall flip a coin to decide which Party strikes the first name and the losing party shall strike the first name. Such procedure shall apply in each case. The Party demanding arbitration shall, within two (2) working days thereafter, with written notice to the other, advice the arbitrator of his selection. (23)

What should be noted first are the contractual time limits that appear in these clauses. Time limitations, particularly ones as brief as these, enable the parties to move their disputes along expeditiously to a conclusion. This is one of the ways in which parties may remedy delays, one of the sources of their own common complaints.

More, as to the reason for citing the above clause: the author was personally involved in the bargaining that led to its adoption. In these particular negotiations, representatives of both parties, company and union, were concerned about the question of which one would strike the first name from an arbitration list. Each party considered it a disadvantage to strike first, and such is reflected by the contractual language.

PROCEDURES

Arbitrators are generally selected on either a case-by-case or a permanent basis. Where the arbitrator is chosen for each case—the ad hoc method we have been reviewing—a wide variety of procedures have been adopted for determining who is to be the impartial umpire. Some parties prefer to leave the selection to an agency such as FMCS or the American Arbitration Association (AAA). While these agencies quite willingly perform such service, they much prefer that the parties themselves make the choice.

Still another method that has been popular with many parties for several years is one that operates as follows:

Each party is supplied with a list of names. Each, independently of the other, eliminates from the list names that are unacceptable to it. Usually, more than one name will not be acceptable, for a variety of real or imagined reasons; and, more often than not, one or more will be acceptable. If two or more names are acceptable to the party, each name is numbered in the order of preference.

When compared, the lists may show something like the following:

Union List		Company List	
	A. Adams	1.	A. Adams
5.	M. Easy		M. Easy
3.	B. Brown	4.	B. Brown
	F. Hard	3.	F. Hard
	L. Baker		L. Baker
1.	S. Smith	5.	S. Smith
	W. Jones		W. Jones
2.	H. White	2.	H. White
4.	C. Black		C. Black

In this example, H. White, S. Smith, and B. Brown are acceptable to both parties, the others having been cancelled by one or the other. By adding the respective ratings, H. White would be the top man on the basis of having received the lowest numerical total (2 + 2 = 4), with S. Smith in second place (1 + 5 = 6), and B. Brown in third place (3 + 4 = 7). The lower the total score of the arbitral candidate, the higher his level of acceptability to both parties, since each party has numbered the candidates in the order of its preference, beginning with 1. Thus the appointment as arbitrator would first be offered to White, after which, if he declined or was otherwise unable to serve, the parties would offer the post to Smith and Brown, respectively.

Obviously, there are shortcomings in this system, just as there are in the others cited. In the procedures previously discussed, the parties are more or less stuck with the appointment made by FMCS or AAA, or with their own selection made by alternately striking names from a preestablished list provided by those agencies. Of course, such lists may be returned to the agencies, by mutual agreement of the parties, if all names listed thereon are wholly unacceptable to either. However, this is a relatively rare occurrence, primarily because of the care and professional approach of FMCS and AAA in their construction of arbitration panels. Usually the parties will merely proceed to check off names.

In this procedure there are a few potential problem areas. There is always a good chance that the parties will coincidentally strike names in a manner that precludes selection from a particular list—that is, each could strike the names that are acceptable to the other. Such a happenstance would necessitate a second list and a repetition of the above-described process, all of which imposes lengthy delay upon the ultimate selection of an arbitrator. Naturally, the same result would occur if either party checked all names on the list. Also, in theory at least, it could happen over and over.

The answer to this dilemma may lie in the parties' agreeing to limit themselves to a maximum number of exclusions—say, three names each from a panel containing seven.

As previously stated, the parties may elect to set up permanent machinery for the determination of disputes. An example of one such arrangement follows:

> Within thirty (30) days after the date of this Agreement, representatives of the parties hereto will obtain from the American Arbitration Association a list of Arbitrators, and will agree upon a panel of three arbitrators, obtaining additional lists, if necessary. The parties shall furnish said Association the names of the arbitrators so selected. Thereafter, the Association shall designate one of said arbitrators to hear each grievance that may be referred to arbitration but no one arbitrator shall hear more than three grievances. If said panel shall be exhausted, representatives of the parties shall in the same manner select a second panel of arbitrators to hear grievances arising thereafter, each of whom may hear not more than three grievances. (24)

Permanent arbitrators or systems providing for them are more frequently found in large enterprises with long collective bargaining histories and which have a large number of cases going into arbitration.

Several arguments are put forward by those favoring permanent-arbitrator systems. It is contended that a permanent arbitrator comes to know the peculiarities of the business better; he understands the features of the relationship which makes it unique to the given parties; his rulings have conformity, continuity, and uniformity, which simplifies enforcement of the contract; and his awards set precedents that form a set of guides and rules supplementing the contract and enabling smoother labor relations.

However, the permanent-arbitrator system is not without its opponents. Labor-relations practitioners may oppose it on the grounds that (1) the arbitrator tends too often to play the role of mediator; (2) he eventually tends to supplement or supplant management in the determination of industrial relations policies; (3) he may because he must please both sides, or comes to feel that he should, have a tendency to decide the issue on the basis of the trend of decisions instead of on the merits of each particular case; and (4) his presence often acts to promote the number of grievances pushed into arbitration.

If one elects to secure a permanent arbitrator, several considerations are advisable. First, one should be extremely thoughtful and thorough in researching and selecting the individual who will serve. It is easier and less painful to avoid making a mistake in selection than to undo and outlive mistaken decisions rendered. Second, one should stay with ad hoc arbitration until one is quite acquainted with the process, how it works, and how various arbitrators reason and function during hearings. Exposure to different arbiters may assist in the later selection of a permanent arbitrator. Third, one should have a clear understanding with the selected permanent umpire with regard to fee arrangements. If a yearly retainer is required, one should take into account the frequency of arbitral cases in the past. What are the charges of the arbitrator? How available is he? Will he readily give his time without unreasonable delay? These are a few of the primary questions one will wish to have answered satisfactorily. Fourth, even if a permanent arbitrator is decided upon, one may wish to consider keeping provisions in the labor agreement which would enable the use and selection of temporary arbitrators and would specify that the clause should apply when the office of the permanent umpire is vacant or when he cannot serve for any reason. It is much better to have taken this precaution before an emergency absence occurs, than to try to cope with it at the very time the need for arbitral help is greatest. The fifth consideration is only applicable to some parties, whose investigation it merits. In a multiplant, or multidivision, operation, one may wish to consider using the same permanent individual under each of several agreements, To pursue this thought one step further, if one's industry has an employers' association, one may wish to consider joining with others to select and retain one umpire, especially if each member of the group feels the need for an arbitrator who understands the peculiarities of the particular industry. As a result, a group may be able to attract and finance with a more sizable retainer an arbiter of wider experience and national reputation. When such arrangements are made, often the parties will name several alternates to serve in the absence of the permanent selection.

Arbitration is a quasi-judicial process. In essence, the purpose of arbitration is the adjudication of disputes by an impartial umpire akin to a judge in a legal action. Unlike a mediator, he does not have to suggest formulas and work out agreements. He merely hears the evidence in a dispute and hands down a decision based on the facts. Arbitrators, unlike judges in legal actions, are not bound by legal rules of evidence or by precedent.

There are a few more reasons why careful selection of a permanent arbitrator is so important. He may conduct a hearing in any manner peculiar to his particular philosophy and style of personality. He may run a tight or loose hearing. He may rule on objections raised on testimony or procedure—disallowing and precluding —or he may receive all testimony and evidence, despite objections to their admission—taking it "for whatever it may later prove to be worth." He may be a strict constructionist in his interpretation of the agreement, ignoring consideration of any factors or matters outside of contract language. Or he may give weight to the customs and practices of the parties, previous arbitration decisions, previous grievance settlements, and the history of collective bargaining discussions between the parties.

It is advisable that matters such as these, and others to be mentioned later, be taken into consideration in the selection of an arbitrator, whether for permanent duty or for ad hoc service.

Arbitration may be conducted either by a single nonpartisan arbitrator or a tripartite board, composed of an equal number of employer and union representatives and an impartial member acting as chairman. A few agreements allow the parties the option of having either a single arbitrator or an arbitration board. In some contracts, the partisan representatives first attempt to settle the disputed issue. Only after they have been unable to agree on a final decision does the board become a tripartite board, with the impartial man added to make a decision possible. Most often, all members of an arbitration board, including the impartial chairman, are selected before the arbitration hearings start, and the board functions as a tripartite board at all times.

Arbitration may be conducted by an individual or a board newly chosen each time a dispute arises, or by a person or board named in the contract and serving continuously for the duration of the agreement.

Agreements calling for permanent arbitration usually specify a single arbitrator rather than a tripartite board. In some instances where a board is provided, only the impartial chairman serves on a permanent basis, while the company and union representatives are selected for each dispute.

Whatever the prescribed procedure, when one is trying to agree on an arbitrator, only the requirements of the labor contract limit the selection. Naturally, if the contract specifies that the arbitrator chosen must come from panels of FMCS or AAA, or be a member of the National Academy, such a requirement, unless mutually waived, dictates at least the source. Otherwise, the company and union may choose anyone they wish to arbitrate for them, and they often obtain their third-party neutral from other sources. It is not unheard of for a priest, minister, rabbi, mayor, other public official —even a governor—to decide an issue for an employer and a union. Parties may even agree upon an apparently partisan person, if such a choice is mutually acceptable. Sometimes the results are acceptable; more often they are at best questionable. The quality of the arbitrator may eventually prove to be as significant as the merits of one's case and the quality of one's presentation at the arbitral hearing.

3

Researching the Arbitrator

A LIST of names of arbitrators has been submitted to each party by the Federal Mediation and Conciliation Service (FMCS) or the American Arbitration Association (AAA), or perhaps has been obtained from some less frequently used source. The list typically contains seven names or five names or some other odd number requested by the parties from one of these services.

The list lies before one of the parties on his desk. Perhaps, if he is lucky, one or two of the names are familiar to him. He may have previously used one (or more) of the arbitrators listed and thus have already had some actual experience with him. He is therefore familiar with the arbitrator's style and the manner in which he conducts a hearing; he has at least some notion of the kind of rationale he employs in arriving at conclusions. If one is fortunate enough for this to be the case, one has somewhat minimized the research chore of sifting through the potential arbiters. Those who go to arbitration often, or on a fairly regular basis, have an edge over others in their familiarity with the professionals in the business of deciding disputes as neutral third parties.

By virtue of their having appeared on previous lists, perhaps one has some knowledge of the background, experience, qualifications, and general reputation of certain names appearing on the list. Presumably, if their names have appeared on previous lists submitted, the arbitrators may have already been checked on in the past. If so, one's chore is further diminished and one fifth or one seventh or more of one's basic questions have already been answered. But if all the names are unfamiliar, what then? Or worse yet, if one does not know what steps to take in order to determine to his satisfaction the arbitrator's qualifications, what then?

Hopefully, this chapter will serve to answer the most basic questions in this regard.

QUALIFICATIONS

In order to serve the parties fairly, an individual must have certain qualities of character. At the moment, I am not reviewing other desirable arbitral qualities, such as experience, knowledge, or education. These will be reviewed shortly.

Among the qualities of character the parties are entitled to find in their selection, none can be considered more important than that of impartiality. It is a fact of life that everyone is possessed of certain biases and prejudices, on an endless variety of matters. It is not possible to find a human who is not. At the same time, it is not unreasonable of the parties to expect to have an individual who will discipline himself to decide the issues on their own merits. Sentiment or bias for or against the issue, a particular party, or the conditions of the parties' labor agreement are factors that must be divorced from the decision-making process. From the opening of the hearing until a decision is rendered, an open mind is not merely desirable, it is essential, not only to provide equity and impartial justice to the parties and their relationship, but also for the preservation of an honorable arbitration profession. There is no implicit suggestion here that arbitrators are not impartial and fair—quite the contrary. The absence of these essential qualities is definitely the exception; that is why arbitration and its neutral professionals have flourished for so many years. Without these qualities of character, found in the overwhelming majority of practicing arbitrators, they and the process they serve would never have endured. This is not to say that an arbiter does not, or even should not, call the shots as he sees them. He must exercise his own best judgment, which sometimes results in the rendering of

an unpopular decision. If such an award is the result of his judgment and not the consequence of partiality or favoritism, he has
still provided a valuable service and has not been guilty of violating
one of the basic and essential precepts of his office. An arbitrator
is not engaged in a popularity contest. Accordingly, while one or
both parties may be displeased with a particular decision, they will
not lose faith in the fundamental benefits of the process so long
as they are convinced that awards are the consequences of judgment impartially exercised.

The integrity of the arbitrator is equally important. The arbitrator does not seek to serve the parties, nor is he elected to the
position he holds. As a consequence, he does not serve or operate
at the sufferance of either party. He has not, nor should he have,
any vested interest in or allegiance to representatives of either
faction. His post has not been a political appointment. His integrity has hopefully been established and is discernible to the parties
through his prior business and personal dealings and affiliations.

To many practitioners in the labor-relations arena, the fact that
an arbitrator has previously gained considerable experience in
representing exclusively either labor or management gives the kiss
of death to the desirability of his serving as a neutral. However,
it simply does not follow as night the day that previous partisan
service renders the individual incapable of impartiality and integrity in functioning as a true neutral. In this respect, labor arbitration is somewhat akin to other fields of endeavor. Many of the best
defense lawyers were previously district attorneys. Many referees
and umpires, engaged in rendering decisions impartially and with
unquestioned integrity, were formerly players in the same game—
baseball, football, basketball, hockey, and the like—and some even
performed for the same teams they later render judgments for and
against. A more reliable determinant of whether the arbitrator's
feelings of partisanship still prevail would be the public record of
the cases he has decided and the manner in which he has decided
them. In fact, that prior partisanship may have been the very instrument by which he has gained the depth and breadth of insight
and experience that enables him to appraise the issues and circumstances with greater understanding. Some of the ablest and most
informed neutrals practicing as labor arbitrators today, with im-
peccable reputations in the eyes of both parties, came out of the
labor movement or from management.

Whether a certain experience or education or training is necessary for all arbiters is questionable. No two possess exactly the same kind or amount of background credentials. But all, irrespective of their lists of experience and background attributes, must possess the essential qualities of character which enable them to render decisions impartially and to serve with unchallengeable integrity.

Let us turn now to another area—that of actual experience and qualifications. There are a few helpful indications.

If the individual is a member of the National Academy of Arbitrators, he is an experienced neutral who has met several high standards imposed by his peers. Perhaps there are no harsher critics than one's own peers, and, if he has passed the scrutiny and investigation of the membership committee of the academy, the odds are substantially good that the arbitrator will possess necessary credentials.

The Academy, however, does not include all the individuals who have impressive qualifications and capabilities as arbitrators. The Academy, founded in 1947, takes in relatively few new members, so that not being on its roster does not any indicate lack of ability or proficiency.

Arbitrators on the panels of FMCS and AAA have also been investigated prior to their acceptance by those agencies. In fact, both agencies require that the individual provide a number of references from the ranks of both labor and management who will attest to his acceptability, knowledge, and character. In addition, his application for membership on these rosters must exhibit sufficient labor-management exposure to qualify him for consideration. Therefore, arbitrators whose names are furnished on such panels have already been screened for impartiality. The rules of nonpartisan arbitration agencies forbid an arbitrator to serve in a case in which he has any financial or personal interest or is related to any of the parties, that is, unless the parties expressly waive this condition in writing.

The qualification of arbitrators becomes doubly important when it is realized that they have been deemed to be judicial officers and share certain immunities from suit by parties, since arbitrators "must be free from the fear of reprisals" and "must of necessity be uninfluenced by any fear of consequences for their acts." (25)

It is not uncommon to hear disparaging remarks, from both

management and labor, about the integrity of arbitrators, their principles, and their biases. This contributes to the unusually troublesome problem of selecting an arbiter.

The usefulness of arbitration in the field of industrial relations is largely the result of the quality of the arbitrators—their personal and professional integrity, their intimate acquaintance with the varied facets of industrial life, and their judgment. The parties themselves are mostly responsible for whatever undermining of arbitration there has been. In their eagerness to win cases, they contribute materially to reducing the usefulness of arbitration and to breeding attitudes of cynicism vis-à-vis arbitration on the part of companies, unions, and the public generally. The foundation stone of successful arbitration is the confidence of the parties in the fairness and competence of the arbitrator. (26)

As mentioned earlier, sometimes the parties will specify certain arbitral qualifications in their labor instrument. For example, the agreement between New Jersey Bell Telephone Company and the Electrical Workers (IBEW), expiring July 20, 1974, contained this clause among its arbitration provisions:

> (3) At the same time that written demand for arbitration is served upon the other party, the American Arbitration Association shall be requested in writing to appoint an impartial chairman. The Impartial shall not be an officer, director, or employee of the company or of any company in the Bell System, nor shall he be a member, officer, official, employee, representative, attorney or counsel of the Union or of any other Union or labor organization.

It is doubtful that such a restriction on AAA need be spelled out in the labor agreement. It is not conceivable that that agency would knowingly submit a panel containing the names of persons from the contractually prohibited categories. However, for whatever reasons, these parties felt more assured with the expressed precautionary measures.

More often, the parties specify in their contract the qualities sought in the arbitrator rather than listing those that would be unacceptable. An example of one such provision follows:

> Within two (2) working days thereafter, the Parties shall jointly write to the Arbitrator selected and request hearing dates. Neither party shall deliberately delay the setting of a hearing date.
> 1. Such arbitrators must be technically qualified to resolve dis-

putes and have skill, knowledge and-or experience relating to measurements of standards of work.

2. Such arbitrators must have prior arbitration experience in regularly deciding issues relating to measurements of standards of work.

C. Any arbitrator selected by the above procedures must be currently a member of the National Academy of Arbitrators. (27)

The above language appears in a contract that contains two grievance and arbitration provisions, one dealing with disputes outside the "wage incentive plan," and the other, quoted in part, dealing with disputes about the administration and implementation of an incentive standards program. It is evident that an attempt has been made here to engage only arbitrators who have industrial engineering expertise, education, and/or experience.

Only relatively few contracts specify eligibility qualifications for arbitrators. As in the above example, only engineers or other technically trained and experienced persons may be allowed to arbitrate disputes involving time-study and incentive systems. Appointment of public officeholders is occasionally prohibited and, in the case of tripartite systems, lawyers may be precluded from serving either party. To prevent selection of an individual whose judgment might somehow be prejudiced from association with the parties involved in the dispute, persons living within a specified distance of the enterprise may be declared ineligible for service as arbitrators. The reverse situation may sometimes be found also: a person familiar with the particular industry may be preferred and so specified by the contract.

There can be no question that substantial arbitration experience is of considerable benefit, both to the arbitrator and to the parties he serves. However, the absence of experience as an arbitrator can be materially compensated for if he possesses a keen and analytical mind and has the ability to quickly grasp and perceive new subject matter presented to him. Competence may be acquired during the course of hearings where parties have adequately prepared and intelligently presented the facts upon which the determination is to be made. The most experienced arbitrator cannot fully understand the issue and the circumstances surrounding it unless these are clearly articulated to him during the proceeding. Of course, integrity either exists or does not exist. When the least question arises about his integrity, the arbitrator's usefulness ceases. This ingredient is the equal of maturity of judgment and both are indispensable.

There are occasions when special knowledge is required about the matter to be decided. Such instances are in the minority, and few have been previously mentioned. In the vast majority of cases, general experience in industrial matters, however obtained, will enable an arbitrator to relate to the issues at hand.

The question of whether an arbitrator needs legal training in order to function adequately and successfully arises frequently. The answer is no. It is true that many arbitrators have been trained in law, just as many practitioners in labor relations have been. It is also true that such training usually operates to the benefit of such individuals. The process of training in legal affairs provides a neutral discipline that promotes objective and analytical thinking. It teaches the evaluation of facts and information, with limitations on personal prejudice. It disciplines toward the elimination of extraneous matters and the consideration of relevant and pertinent factors only. It is also true that several of the ablest established arbitrators have law backgrounds. However, it is equally true that many of the most able, best established, and most reputable arbitrators have not had legal training. Finally, it has to be recognized that not all legally trained individuals make good arbitrators.

It was stated earlier that legal training *usually* operates to the benefit of the individual. But not always. The arbitrator's legal background may even be a hindrance to a full and open hearing of all matters. The arbitration process is only quasi-judicial, and strict rules of evidence, testimony, and procedure do not apply. One of the virtues of the process is its availability and suitability to the parties as a fast and relatively simple means of resolving their differences. The introduction of too much "legalese" into the system may actually complicate it unduly for those it is intended to serve. It may stifle both their informal presentations of their cases and their dispositions toward the subsequent use of the process. How a man reasons and exercises good judgment, how he analyzes and evaluates situations, and how much objectivity and adherence to facts he demonstrates are far more important considerations than what formal education he may have obtained.

How the parties determine the presence or absence of these essential qualities will be reviewed next.

EVALUATION OF ARBITRAL CANDIDATES

The Bureau of National Affairs (BNA) (1231 25th Street, N.W., Washington, D.C.) publishes *Labor Arbitration Reports,* which are designed to provide accurate and authoritative information about arbitration awards. They also contain information about particular arbitrators, including their names, addresses, telephone numbers, birth dates, training, positions, affiliations, and publications. Access to these volumes, or to those provided by other such reporting services, are invaluable tools to the practitioner wishing to examine the published decisions of certain arbitrators. One word of caution is in order. Not all decisions of all arbitrators are published—only a very small percentage are. Not all decisions of any particular arbitrator are published for public review. Arbitrators choose only certain cases to submit to the publishing services. These reporting services must also be selective in the cases they publish. The factors of space and expense are obvious determinants. Therefore, published arbitration reports are somewhat like an iceberg, only a small portion of which is visible to the examiner. The great majority never get into print, primarily because of the limiting factors mentioned. In addition, the arbitrator must obtain permission from the parties before submitting a report to one of the publications. Nevertheless, a sizable number are available to the interested and diligent researcher.

The increasing frequency of arbitration awards, both in number and significance, led BNA to a decision to segregate the text of all court decisions relating to labor arbitration into separate volumes. It devotes the space saved thereby in *Labor Arbitration Reports* to increased coverage of labor arbitration awards. These volumes and the *Index-Digest,* particularly, contain the aforementioned "Directory of Arbitrators." This publication also furnishes a full listing of the unions involved in the reported cases, providing the popular name of the union and the official name of the national or international union and its subordinate branches.

Such service is merely the launching pad for someone wishing to learn more about a prospective arbiter. Consulting these publications is one of the essential steps to be taken if a thorough and comprehensive job of research is to be accomplished. There are other equally productive sources.

Additional information regarding arbitrators' qualifications may also be obtained by turning to the *Who's Who* (of arbitrators) put out by Prentice-Hall, Inc. (Englewood Cliffs, New Jersey). From this source one can learn the potential arbitrator's age, address, education, occupation, affiliations, experience, books or articles written (often informative and insightful as to labor-relations concepts and philosophy), awards published, and a variety of other miscellaneous information.

Commerce Clearing House (CCH) (4025 West Peterson Avenue, Chicago, Illinois 60646), is another major publisher of decisions. Its volumes entitled *American Labor Arbitration Awards (ALAA)* provide a comprehensive reporting of hundreds of awards. This series is not a duplication of the BNA service. True, cases published by CCH may also be found in BNA's *Labor Arbitration Reports,* but there are many reported by one which are not necessarily published by the other.

Both services are equally impressive, and parties generally choose between them on the basis of which is more appealing in terms of reporting style and ease in locating desired matters therein. If both sets of volumes are available, the dedicated researcher may find it is well worth his time to examine in each the reported cases that pertain to his particular potential arbitral candidate.

The panels maintained by AAA and FMCS contain the names of hundreds of qualified arbitrators. Whenever either of these agencies receive a request for an arbitrator, or a panel of arbiters, a listing is submitted. Such a list includes several pertinent particulars on each of the individuals offered. A hypothetical sample of the type of biographical data included follows:

Harold Decisive
Occupation: Professor of Economics and Chairman, Department of
    Economics
Address: (Bus.) Ohio State University
                Columbus, Ohio
           (Res.) 1050 Treelined Street
                Columbus, Ohio
Telephone: West 6–7689   East 2–3804
Arbitration experience: Arbitrator since 1952. Majority of working
    time devoted to teaching, with balance spent in arbitration.
    Has experience in arbitration of wages, fringe benefits, griev-
    ances concerning management prerogatives, overtime and

premium pay, job specifications, seniority, discipline, and discharge.

Other experience: Twenty-four years teaching experience. Labor-relations consultant, Atomic Energy Commission, 1954–57. Mediator, U.S. Conciliation Service, 1945–47. Corps of Engineers, U.S. Army, 1942–45.

Professional affiliations: American Arbitration Association, Industrial Relations Research Association, American Economics Association

Education: B.A., M.A., Ph.D.

Date of birth: March 6, 1912

Per diem fee: Not exceeding $150

This hypothetical data sheet, representative of the type and form of material that both AAA and FMCS forward to requesting parties, is taken from the format of FMCS.

Some parties with arbitration pending make their determinations on the basis of these sheets. While they are helpful and informative in themselves, the data sheets should only be the basis for further investigation. At this point, one of the recommended things to do is to turn to the aforementioned publications of BNA and CCH. At the same time, one may wish to ask AAA or FMCS for the names of parties who have been previously served by the arbitrator(s) one is interested in, and get from them an evaluation of the arbitrator's performance.

Employer associations and chambers of commerce, too, can sometimes furnish lists of cases decided by arbitrators of the locality.

One should find out how many times the same parties have chosen the particular candidate; "repeat orders" are a strong endorsement.

As many as possible of the people who have arbitrated cases before the candidate should be contacted. A suggested list of questions is given below. One should try to pin them down to specific good or bad actions or qualities, remembering, nevertheless, that anyone who has lost a case may be inclined to blame the arbitrator. On the other hand, a recommendation from the losing party or a criticism from the party given the award has special weight.

After the prospective client has talked with other parties and read opinions, he should judge the arbitrator on the general quality of his work—not on how many cases he has decided for one side or the other. If the majority of his awards favor the union, this does not necessarily indicate a pro-union bias, since a great many variables enter the picture.

There are many questions that may be raised with parties who have already had experience with the candidate under consideration. The following are merely a few of the more pertinent ones:

- How soon after the close of the hearing was the award submitted? Was it within the preferred 30 days? If not, was there a justifiable reason for it taking longer?
- What was the issue decided?
- Did the arbitrator consider only the relevant contractual provision, or did he give weight to other matters, such as the practices and customs of the parties, the history of collective bargaining on the disputed clauses, etc.?
- Did the arbitrator follow the concept that management rights are residual, that all rights and privileges of managing the business continue to reside with the employer except to the extent they have been abridged or compromised in provisions of the contract?
- How did he conduct the hearing? Was it informal or legalistic?
- Did the arbitrator prefer a transcript of the hearing and the use of a court stenographer, or did he record the events of the hearing by making his own notes?
- Did he rule on objections, or did he accept all evidence and testimony proferred by the parties?
- Did he ask many questions of the company, the union, and their witnesses, or did he let what was given him suffice?
- In the "opinion" portion of his award, were his remarks pertinent and on point with the issue to be decided, or did he delve into extraneous and foreign matters that were not submitted or intended to elicit his opinion?
- Was his opinion and award clear and understandable?
- What were his charges? Were they considered reasonable in light of the length of the hearing(s) and the complexity of the case?

The reason for asking most of these questions is fairly evident. They deal with the arbitrator's promptness, style, objectivity, analytical ability, rationale, and fees. These are all important considerations. Merely learning this much about a man may give one party a decided edge on the other if it has not been equally resourceful. It may have an influence on the approach to be taken and manner to be followed. It may enable a party to prepare its witnesses as to what to expect. It may provide it with insights into an arbitrator's personal idiosyncracies. The arbitrator may be more expensive than anticipated, although other positive determinations may outweigh this factor. It may be discovered that he is inclined to go far afield in his "opinion" even when he renders a favorable award. Such a discovery may lead to the realization that one could "win the battle but lose the war." Needless to say, one may decide to reject a candidate for a particular case. Despite such a decision, he may be considered acceptable for some future issue.

These are all important reasons for engaging in the research. They are not the only reasons. A subsequent chapter contains a review of several representative arbitral conclusions. An attempt is made to examine certain critical issues that appear frequently before arbitrators. The coverage is not intended to be all-inclusive of the wide variety of disputes that enter the arbitration process. That degree of comprehensive reporting is left to the able services already mentioned. However, an attempt is made, in selected critical areas, to show that there is some divergent arbitral opinion about such matters as subcontracting, discipline and discharge, management rights, past practice, work rules, violations of no-strike pledges, and others. Although there are many settled and well-established concepts endorsed by the majority of arbitrators, there are other areas where some difference of opinion persists, even among the best known, most reputable neutrals. Once this is realized, additional reasons, which are perhaps more important than those already cited, emerge for researching a prospective arbitrator.

Whatever the findings at the end of the research, they should not be disposed of. Instead an arbitration file should be developed and maintained in order to accumulate all of the information pertinent to the selection, evaluation, and qualifications of arbitrators. Some candidates' names will appear time and again on lists submitted, particularly if the party is involved with any sizable frequency in using the process. If one wants others in the labor-management community to share opinions with him, the willingness must be reciprocal. If a party has *justifiable* cause to be dissatisfied with the service of a particular arbitrator, he should share his concern in a fair and objective manner with the agency providing his name. If criticism is constructively expressed and intended, the agency will be grateful for the report. If it sees an appraisable pattern of comments from different parties, that will enable it to determine appropriate reaction if necessary. Preserving the results of research can save one the considerable time, trouble, and expense of later having to duplicate his efforts. In addition, the implications of the divergent arbitral conclusions on certain critical issues should be considered. (This subject will be subsequently reviewed in brief.) They may indicate whether a particular candidate comes from one school of thought or another and whether he would serve the best interests of a specific case.

4

Representative Arbitration Clauses

LET us first take a statistical look at the general restrictions that parties customarily place upon the arbitrator.

Restraints upon the arbitrator appear in more than three fifths of all arbitration provisions. Most of these (88 percent) contain the general restriction that the arbitrator may not alter or add to the contract. More than one fifth of the arbitration provisions specifically rule out arbitration of general wage issues. About 8 percent specifically exclude production standards; this exclusion is a common practice in the transportation (automobile) industry. Two percent of the arbitration clauses forbid arbitration of safety and health issues, one half of these are found in the contracts of transportation-equipment companies (28).

A significant number of arbitration agreements limit the retroactivity of the arbitrator's award, usually to the date on which the grievance was first formally presented to management.

AUTHORITY OF ARBITRATORS

The most common limitations appearing in labor contracts prohibit the arbiter from adding to, subtracting from, or otherwise modifying the agreement: he is usually confined to questions involving the application or interpretation of the contract itself. The following contract clauses are representative of those that place a rather tight rein on the arbiter's power:

46. No matter, other than a grievance which is an alleged violation of a specific provision as written and expressed in this agreement, can be reviewed on its merits by the arbitrator. If the grievance does not meet the aforementioned standard and involves a matter outside of the expressed terms of this Agreement and is not specifically covered by a written provision of this Agreement, the arbitrator shall refrain from reviewing the merits of the grievance. In such cases, the arbitrator shall deny the grievance on the basis of the last answer given in the 3rd Step of the Grievance Procedure as set forth in Article IV, Section 3, of this Agreement. The Parties agree to follow the Arbitration Procedure in accordance with the time limits and conditions contained therein.

47. The Arbitrator shall have no authority to add to, subtract from, modify, change or alter in any way the provisions of this Agreement or any amendment, or supplement thereto, as written and expressed, or to extend its duration unless the Parties have agreed in writing to give him specific authority to do so.

48. The arbitrator shall arrive at his decision solely upon the facts, evidence and contentions as presented by the Parties during the arbitration proceeding.

49. The arbitrator shall not consider any evidence which was not introduced by the Parties in the Steps of the Grievance Procedure as set forth herein. (29)

This happens to be another provision that the author was instrumental in establishing in the course of collective bargaining. In the majority of instances, it is the union that is most interested in broadening the scope of the arbitral forum. It often seeks, and many agreements contain, contractual provisions that state that "any dispute" or "any misunderstanding" or "any disagreement" shall be subject to the grievance and arbitration processes. Naturally, where such a broad definition exists, it may enable a party to use the grievance and arbitration procedures to gain additional measures, benefits, or conditions that were not obtained during collective bargaining. As mentioned previously it may even allow a party to seek and attain through this means, advantages that it did not even attempt to achieve while negotiating the agreement.

The employer, on the other hand, usually wishes to keep the scope of the grievance and arbitration clauses narrow and specific. In most cases, the company wishes to limit the arbitration process, as well as the grievance procedure, if possible, to those matters that are expressly provided for in the contract. Of course, wanting and achieving are two different things; to obtain specific and unequivocal contract language in this regard is often easier said than done.

Despite their divergent objectives, it is often in the best interests of both parties, union and company, to provide some limitations on the arbitrator's jurisdiction. There are occasions when such restrictions benefit the union as well as the employer. The fact is that many disputes go to arbitration which should not. The reasons are numerous and varied. Although many disputes go to arbitration because of honest disagreements over contract terms, many go for political reasons: either union or management feels compelled, for some reason, to make a case of something that is really of little consequence.

A collectively bargained contract is rarely a rational document; imprecise terms, variously understood, creep in; words whose meanings the parties seem to agree upon in negotiations tend to become vague and subject to whatever interpretation a grievant, union spokesman, or company representative later chooses to make of them. The result is certainly similar to a political issue.

There are occasions when a particular employee or group of employees will raise a grievance claim that has nothing whatsoever to do with the terms and provisions of the contract, but deals instead with some irrelevant or extraneous matter. It is possible also that such a specious claim is not endorsed by the union and that the union does not wish to provide it with arbitral support. In fact, an arbitral decision in favor of some such grievance can operate to the immediate or eventual detriment of the union's interests. Just as management does not want an arbitrator to add to or expand its meanings or intendments beyond what the employer has already conceded, neither does the union want him to subtract from or alter intended commitments so as to cause loss of negotiated gains.

Turning now to actual cases in which contract language circumscribed the powers of the arbitrator, how have arbitrators themselves functioned within its perimeters? A few sample opinions follow.

A union's grievance concerned an employer's method of recalling employees back to work after a strike. This occurred under a contract that limited arbitration to differences arising between the employer and the union, or any employee, "concerning the interpretation, application, or compliance with the provisions of this agreement" and further stated that the arbitrator "shall have no authority to amend, modify, alter, subtract from, or add to" the contract. The seniority rules of the contract referrred *only* to posting and were not expressly applicable to the recall of employees following a strike. In addition, an alleged oral agreement to recall strikers in order of seniority could not be considered or interpreted by the arbiter under the written contract's limiting arbitration provision and its clauses barring additions or amendments to the agreement. (30) Accordingly, arbitrator Sidney A. Wolff ruled that the dispute was not arbitrable.

Another arbitration decision, which was subsequently upheld in court involved a union that had alleged that the employer had violated the agreement by contracting out work. It was held that the union was not entitled to arbitration of this claim because (1) a mere allegation that a contract had been violated did not automatically entitle the union to arbitration under a clause providing for arbitration of "alleged provisions" of the contract; (2) no provision expressly covered subcontracting, even though the parties did bargain on it; and (3) the contract specified that the company would bargain on matters not covered by the contract, but might refuse to arbitrate any such matter. (31) Again, it was ruled that such a grievance under this type of clause was not arbitrable.

Still another dispute over subcontracting had to do with an agreement that included a clause providing that "the company has the right to subcontract and designate the work to be performed by the company and the places where it is to be performed, *which right shall not be subject to arbitration.*" Under such a contract, the union disputed the transfer of certain production work to another of the company's plants, where the work would be outside the bargaining jurisdiction of the union. The arbitrator held, and a court later concurred, that the dispute was not arbitrable since it was specifically excluded from arbitration by the aforementioned provision. (32) Again, this result was obtained because the scope of the arbitrable issues had been narrowed.

It should be stated that arbitrators do not use such limits on their powers to avoid facing and dealing with issues they think legitimately fall within their purview.

Under another contract, the arbitration language expressly forbade an arbitrator from adding to its contents. Nevertheless, arbitrator James V. Altieri ruled that he had authority to determine that certain classes of employees were covered by the contract and subject to its provisions, including the union-security clause, even though the parties had failed to negotiate a wage rate for those classifications. In doing so, he was not adding to the contract but was merely interpreting the contract's recognition clause, which expressly related the contract unit to the appropriate unit as defined in the National Labor Relations Board certification. It was ruled that that certification, and not the list of classifications contained in the wage appendix, determined which employees were covered. (33) In this case the limitations on arbitral authority did not preclude an award favoring the union.

The scope of arbitration under a given agreement depends basically on two interrelated factors: (1) the contents of the agreement itself and (2) the authority granted the arbitrator. Any two agreements may limit the arbitrator's authority in identical fashion—for example, to disputes over the interpretation or application of any clause in the agreements. One arbitrator, nevertheless, may have greater scope because the agreement under which he functions covers many more matters than the other. The issues that are arbitrable, therefore, vary with the contents of the agreements themselves.

EXCLUSION OF ISSUES

Some labor agreements modify the basic area of arbitration by specifically excluding certain issues, while others expand on it by explicitly making arbitrable certain issues that are ordinarily beyond this scope. Some agreements are ambiguous about the types of controversies that can be arbitrated. They do not, for example, make clear whether an arbitrator may rule on questions that are not specifically covered by the contract. Some agreements specifically provide that any dispute over wages, hours, or other conditions of employment are subject to arbitration, while others may restrict arbitration to the interpretation of wage and other clauses in the agreement; still others may permit the actual wages or hours as such to be arbitrated. Subjects frequently excluded from arbitration are so-called management prerogatives: production standards, setting rates on new or changed jobs, promotion to a job outside the bargaining unit, and such basic management functions as determining the methods of production. (34)

To provide a better understanding of the various contractual arrangements that have been mentioned generally, it is necessary to take a look at a number of specific provisions.

The labor agreement between Firestone Tire and Rubber Company and the United Rubber Workers union reads as follows:

> The impartial arbitrator or board of arbitration shall have no power to add to, subtract from or modify any provision of this agreement or any supplementary agreement negotiated at the plant level. It is understood that matters involving the general wage scale or differentials in the base rates for pieceworkers and maximum daywork rates for dayworkers which are established at the effective date of this agreement shall not be a subject for arbitration.

Here is a clause that first limits the arbitrator's powers and then goes on to specifically preclude certain issues from access to the arbitration process.

What can be the result if the language is ambiguous or susceptible to more than one interpretation? It has been held that if the arbitration clause arguably embraces the dispute, arbitration will undoubtedly be ordered. The courts have strongly impressed such a thesis in the previously cited cases called the "Steelworkers Trilogy." In the first of these, the contract read:

> Any disputes, misunderstandings, differences or grievances arising between the parties as to the meaning, interpretation and application of the provisions of this agreement . . . may be submitted to the Board of Arbitration for decision. . . . The arbitrator may interpret this agreement and apply it to the particular case under consideration but shall, however, have no authority to add to, subtract from, or modify the terms of the agreement. Disputes relating to discharges or such matters as might involve a loss of pay for employees may carry an award of back pay in whole or in part as may be determined by the Board. . . . The decision of the Board . . . shall be final and conclusively binding. (35)

Another clause in this contract provided that the employer retain various management rights, including the right to direct the work force and to discharge employees for efficiency reasons, while still another provided that workers be retained and promoted on the basis of seniority in cases in which ability and efficiency were equal.

An employee was injured, claimed compensation benefits (his physician rated him as 25 percent disabled), and then asserted his seniority right to his job. The employer refused to arbitrate; the employee sued to compel arbitration; and both the federal district court and the court of appeals ruled against the employee. The court of appeals called the grievance "frivolous, patently baseless . . . not subject to arbitration."

The case went to the Supreme Court, which ruled that the function of the courts is only to determine whether the party seeking arbitration is making a claim that, on its face value, is governed by the contract, not to determine the merits of a grievance under the guise of interpreting the arbitration clause of the contract. Since the dispute between the parties had been about the meaning, interpretation, and application of the contract, arbitration should have been ordered, the Supreme Court held.

In the leading case of the three, between Warrior and Gulf Navigation Company and the United Steelworkers of America, the disputed contract provision read as follows:

> Should differences arise between the company and the Union or its members . . . as to the meaning and application of the provisions of this Agreement, or should any local trouble of any kind arise, there shall be no suspension of work on account of such differences, but an earnest effort shall be made to settle such differences in the following manner [by the grievance and arbitration procedure]. (36)

The contract also included a provision that excluded strictly management functions from arbitration. The employer contracted out work and subsequently—in part as a result—laid off some bargaining-unit employees. The federal district court and the court of appeals upheld the employer's refusal to arbitrate the union's grievance, ruling that contracting out work was within the management function. But the United States Supreme Court sent the matter to arbitration on the grounds that, while the question of arbitrability was for the courts to decide, as Justice Douglas wrote for the majority: "An order to arbitrate should not be denied unless it may be said with positive assurance that the arbitration clause is not susceptible of an interpretation that covers the asserted dispute. Doubts should be resolved in favor of coverage."

The limitation of the court's role in arbitration and the concurrent stress on the contractual agreement to arbitrate differences rather than to strike or lock out out have created controversy about whether to and how to restrict the scope and volume of arbitration.

The Court also ruled, in *United Steelworkers of America v. Warrior and Gulf Navigation Company,* that section 301 of the Labor Management Relations Act (LMRA) assigned to the courts the duty of determining whether the reluctant party had breached its promise to arbitrate. On this point it stated that arbitration "is a matter of contract and a party cannot be required to submit to arbitration any dispute which he has not agreed to so to submit." Thus, such issues as, for example, subcontracting, incentive standards, wages, pension and insurance plans, and discipline and discharge may be excluded from arbitral review, *if* the contractual language clearly and explicitly bars them. But the wording must be unmistakable, since the Supreme Court also ruled that matters should be considered susceptible to arbitration unless expressly excluded.

Among the possible exclusions, discipline and discharge exceptions are perhaps the least prevalent.

In 1969 BNA reported on contractual provisions in 400 separate labor agreements involving a variety of employers and unions. (37) While the survey revealed that 82 percent of these representative contracts expressly stipulated some grounds for discharge, with a general statement that discharge could be made for "just cause" or "cause" appearing in 71 percent of the agreements, the great majority provided for arbitral consideration of discipline and discharge disputes. This is the case, despite the fact, or perhaps just as probably because of it, that discharge and discipline continue to be the issues most frequently submitted to arbitration.

The reactions of the parties to the Trilogy decisions were probably predictable. Management has attempted to broaden its management-prerogatives clause and further narrow the grievance and arbitration provisions. The unions, on the other hand, continue to seek what has always been their objective—but are now further impelled by legal incentive—to erode and reduce those areas that have typically comprised management's functions and broaden further the avenues leading into the arbitration process.

The review of one more case will provide additional helpful

insight. The labor agreement between the Mosaic Tile Company, Zanesville, Ohio, plant, and the Glass and Ceramic Workers Union reads as follows:

> The arbitrator shall only have jurisdiction and authority to interpret the agreement and apply it to the cases presented to him. He shall not change or modify this agreement, or have any authority in the making of a new agreement. He shall have no authority over wage rates established by this agreement, but shall have authority to arbitrate such wage rates, bonus rates and values, or incentive rates as involve changes of method or new operations or new or changed jobs arising during the period of this agreement.

When an incentive plan—negotiated by the company and the union—failed to yield 20 percent above base hourly rates as contemplated, the union demanded back pay to make up the difference.

An arbitrator considered two main questions: (1) Were the disputed rates established by this agreement," and thus excluded from arbitration? (2) If so established, did they come under the exception in the above clause by involving changes of method or new operations?

The union claimed that the rates were arbitrable under the clause because they were not "established by this agreement," but by the company alone. To this, the arbitrator replied that the company had fixed the incentive rates, but only pursuant to an agreement incorporated in the current contract. The rates, then, had to be considered "established by this agreement" and, according to the above clause, removed from his jurisdiction unless the specified exceptions applied.

On this point, the arbitrator rejected the union's contention that the fixing of an incentive rate was a "change in method." Thus, the exception to the limitation on his jurisdiction—"authority to arbitrate such wage rates, bonus rates and values, or incentive rates as involve changes in method"—did not apply in this case. (38)

Whether one should agree with this arbitral conclusion is a moot question. Nevertheless, several educational benefits can be derived from it. First, it reveals how some arbitrators interpret contract language. Next, it points up the importance of careful construction in the drafting of contract clauses. More specific wording might have made the conclusion in this case less doubtful. Finally, it shows again the importance of careful arbitrator selection so as to improve one's odds to whatever extent possible.

ENCOMPASSING ALL ISSUES

As mentioned earlier, some labor agreements expand the basic area of arbitration by making arbitrable certain issues not ordinarily within its scope. This is illustrated in the following clause from the labor agreement between the National Dress Manufacturers Association, Inc. and the Ladies' Garment Workers Union:

> All complaints, disputes or grievances arising between the parties hereto involving questions of interpretation or application of any clause of this agreement, or any acts, conduct or relations between the parties or their respective members, directly or indirectly, shall be submitted in writing by the party hereto claiming to be aggrieved to the other party hereto, and the manager of the association and the Manager of the Joint Council, or their deputies, shall, in the first instance, jointly investigate such complaints, grievances or disputes and attempt an adjustment. Decisions reached by the managers or their deputies shall be binding on the parties hereto. Should they fail to agree, the question or dispute shall be referred to a permanent umpire to be known as the "impartial chairman" in the industry and his decision shall be final and binding upon the parties thereto.

It is further interesting that elsewhere in this agreement the arbitrator is specifically given broad powers, including the authority to fine employers for contract violations, to examine their books, and also to adjust piece rates. These are rather broad discretionary powers to have invested in an arbiter but, for reasons evidently sufficient to the association, this industry chose to do so.

Let us turn now to certain court interpretations of clauses providing for arbitration of "all questions regarding a new contract and scale."

A contract between Potter Press and the International Printing Pressmen read as follows: "It is also agreed that all questions regarding a new contract and scale to become effective at the expiration of this agreement, which cannot be settled by conciliation, shall be decided by arbitration as provided, and this agreement shall remain in force until all differences are settled by conciliation or arbitration." This particular agreement provided a detailed arbitration procedure for unresolved differences on "all questions" affecting the contract and scale, making this procedure the only means of resolving disputes (in effect, banning strikes and lockouts), and waived all rights and remedies otherwise available. But the U.S. court of appeals at Boston held that an agreement to arbitrate terms of a future contract is not enforceable in a federal court. This ruling upheld a lower court decision, which drew a line between using an arbitrator as a judge and using him as a lawmaker. While courts may enforce the "quasi-judicial" function of an arbitrator on an existing contract, neither the Taft-Hartley Act nor the Arbitration Act permits courts to enforce the "quasi-legislative" function of building a new contract. (39)

Another case involved the issue of whether a wage reopener could be arbitrated. The contract provided that: "it shall be the duty of the Adjustment Board to consider all complaints and disputes arising under the terms of this Agreement. (40) A state court found such arbitration enforceable. The agreement also provided for a reopener "limited to the negotiating of an increase of five (5) cents per hour." The union gave notice of reopening, negotiations were held, and no agreement was reached. The union sought arbitration, the employer refused, and, under California state law, the union obtained a court order for arbitration. In the subsequent arbitral hearing, the arbitrator awarded a five-cent increase. The California District Court of Appeals of the First District affirmed a judgment enforcing the award. It held that an arbitrable issue was presented by the union's claim that the parties were required to negotiate to a conclusion under the reopener or submit the dispute to arbitration. Since the dispute was arbitrable, the court held, the arbiter had the power to award the increase even though one had not been promised. (41)

As mentioned previously, the majority of agreements allow for arbitral consideration of disciplinary matters. An excellent example is the following: "The corporation delegates to the Umpire full discretion in cases of discipline for violation of shop rules, or discipline for violation of the Strikes, Stoppages and Lock-outs Section of the Agreement." This is particularly interesting for two reasons. First, the language comes from a contract between General Motors Corporation and the United Auto Workers Union. Second, delegating the employer's disciplinary discretion to an arbitrator for employee violations of the no-strike pledge is not a common occurrence. A more typical provision is the following, which in the contract is directly preceded by the promise not to strike:

> If any individual employee or group of employees violates the previous paragraph [no-strike clause], he or they may be summarily dealt with by the company, at its discretion, by reprimand, layoff without pay, suspension, demotion, or discharge, and any appeal to the Grievance Procedure relative to such action by the Company shall be limited as to whether or not the employee did violate Section 1 of this Article. The Parties agree that discharge is an appropriate penalty for a violation of Section 1 of this article in any case, but this shall not be interpreted to preclude reinstatement and restoration of seniority with back pay in a case where it is established that the discharged employee did not in fact engage in or participate in a violation of Section 1 of this Article. (42)

Most employers seem to favor a provision comparable to the one above. The purpose, of course, is, hopefully, to prevent arbitral consideration of the type of penalty assessed by the company against employees who are accused of breaching the no-strike pledge. The concept here is that the arbitrator determine only the guilt or innocence of the accused party and not whether, in his opinion the punishment fits the crime. It is further intended to permit the company to impose different penalties, of varying types or degrees, against different employees for different alleged violations. Therefore, if the employer proves to the satisfaction of the arbitrator that the employee participated in the manner charged, the arbitrator must uphold the company's action, whatever its nature.

This type of restriction of the arbitrator's discretionary powers is not generally applied to discipline or discharge cases resulting from violations of established shop rules. It is, however, a quite common restriction on arbitral power when discipline results from the breach of a no-strike promise. The reason for this lies in a fundamental element in the relationship between the parties.

The basic promise a union can give to an employer in return for the many promises it receives in a labor agreement, is that there will be no strikes. The right to strike is the union bargaining tool; not to avail itself of that measure is the only thing it has to offer in return for the agreement. Unless this single promise flows from the bargaining agent to the employer, the labor contract cannot be considered a true bilateral exchange of promises.

The grievance and arbitration provisions through which the union may seek and obtain future relief is the quid pro quo for the union's no-strike pledge. In other words, when management obtains from the union a no-strike promise, the union is surrendering its chief economic weapon in order to gain its contractual or extracontractual objectives. In return, management provides a contractual substitute—the grievance and arbitration procedure—which becomes the peaceful, orderly, and expeditious process through which the union can obtain remedy and relief from improper management actions.

When illegal work stoppages occur in breach of this agreement, the union or the employees are again unlawfully resorting to the use of the very economic force that presumably had been harnessed for the term of the contract. When this happens, the bargain is broken and management is not enjoying the guarantee of uninterrupted operations. (43) Management generally wishes to deal with violators sternly and does not wish to have an arbitrator who would be tempted to substitute his judgment for that of the employer with regard to severity of penalty.

One other area of contractual limitation or arbitral discretion should be dealt with here—retroactive adjustments. Many agreements specify that adjustments reached at any stage of the grievance procedure will be applied retroactively to the date of the grievance processing. In other agreements, adjustments are retroactive to the date of occurrence of the action or situation that gave rise to the grievance rather than to the date of presentation; and in still others, to any date mutually agreed upon by the union and the employer. Often the retroactive adjustment is limited to a specified maximum, for example, 30 days. One such clause might read:

> The Company shall not be required to pay back wages more than two (2) days beyond the date a written grievance is filed: Provided, however, that in the case of a pay shortage of which the employee could not have been aware before receiving his pay, adjustments may be made retroactive to the beginning of the pay period covered by such pay, if the employee files his grievance within two (2) working days after receipt of such pay. . . . All claims for back wages

shall be limited to the amount of wages that the employees would otherwise have earned, less any unemployment or other compensation that he may have received from any source during the period of back pay. . . . No decision of an arbitrator shall require further retroactive wage adjustment.

This language appears to be clear in its limitations on retroactive adjustment, at least as far as the question of back wages is concerned.

However, it is important to consider what can result when the contract does not clearly prohibit certain types of relief. While under contract at the International Paper Company, employees were denied work under a given seniority provision. The employer admitted his error and offered the workers the opportunity to make up lost overtime at a later date. The arbitrator held, however, that the employees were entitled to back pay, ruling that, in the absence of contract provisions specifically limiting his authority, back-pay awards were the logical and reasonable means of redressing violations. He also opined that considerations of equity had no proper place in an arbitrator's consideration of contract interpretation. (44)

Under another agreement, which provided that "the findings and decision of the arbitrator shall be conclusive of the controversy submitted, and the decision shall be final and binding on both parties," the umpire ruled that he possessed authority to make a back-pay award in the absence of a provision to the contrary. (45) This has been the arbitral conclusion in a great many cases, the bulk of those embracing the concept. (46)

On an issue over subcontracting, arbitrator Ronald W. Haughton stated that it was customary to award damages in cases in which the employer was found to have violated contractual restrictions on such action. However, none were awarded in this case. Since the union had not specifically requested them in its grievance, it was assumed that it had not intended to do so, and the request for damages made at the hearing was denied. (47)

Last but not least among this sampling of cases involving limitations on arbitral relief is the following. The contract at the Sohio Chemical Company provided that in resolving grievances filed by the union at the third step of the grievance procedure the arbitrator could not award "compensation, damages or other redress to any employee." An arbiter ruled here that he could properly direct two employees who traded jobs in violation of the contract to return to jobs they had held before the trade. He interpreted the term "redress," as used in the contract, as pertaining to money awards to employees who might have been wronged by some improper action of the employer, and not as applicable to or limiting on his arbitral authority to order such action. (48)

After a careful reading of the many published decisions, a fairly well-established principle appears in the absence of a clear and unequivocal restriction to the contrary, arbitrators consider it within their power to award various types of relief—back pay, damages, and corrective measures. In exercising this latitude, of course, they are careful to operate within the confines and constraints of the other contractual clauses.

5

Grievance Procedure

THE grievance machinery is the formal process by which the parties attempt to resolve their differences in a peaceful, orderly, and expeditious manner before resorting to arbitration. As a problem-solving, dispute-settling instrument within the labor agreement, it provides the means whereby an employee can, without jeopardizing his job, express a complaint about his work or working conditions and obtain a fair hearing through progressively higher levels of management.

Under collective bargaining, four important and related features have been added to this concept. (1) While drastically limiting the area of legitimate complaints by establishing the basic conditions of employment and rules for day-to-day administration deemed to be fair by mutual agreement, the collective-bargaining contract may at the same time create a source of grievance and disagreements through ambiguities of language and omissions with regard to circumstances and violations. (2) The union is recognized and accepted as the spokesman for the aggrieved worker, and an inability to agree on a resolution of the issue becomes a dispute between union and management. (3) Because an unresolved grievance becomes a union-management dispute, ultimately a way must be found to reach settlements short of a strike or lockout or substitute for such actions. Final and binding arbitration is the principal means to this end. (4) The procedure for adjusting grievances and grievance disputes is itself spelled out in the agreement and, along with other aspects of collective bargaining, tends to become increasingly formal.

A major union objective in collective bargaining has been the establishment and regulation of such procedures for handling grievances.

Such grievance procedures permit the company and the union to investigate and discuss their problems without interrupting the continued, orderly operation of the business. When the machinery works effectively, it can satisfactorily resolve the overwhelming majority of disputes between the parties.

At present, grievance procedures are found in virtually 99 percent of all labor agreements. The percentage of contracts that provide for arbitration as the terminal point is nearly as high. The almost universal adoption of grievance procedures and grievance arbitration has given rise to the notion, apparently widely held, that strikes or lockouts arising during the terms of the agreements are universally outlawed.

Not quite. A study based on an analysis of 1,717 collective-bargaining agreements, each covering 1,000 workers or more, representing almost all agreements of this size in the United States, exclusive of railroad, airline, and government agreements, established that an *absolute* ban on strikes and lockouts during the term of the agreement appeared in about 45 percent of the contracts. In general, in the absence of an absolute ban on strikes and lockouts, a work stoppage may occur if (1) no grievance procedure is provided, (2) no final and binding arbitration is provided, (3) certain issues are nonarbitrable, (4) certain issues are excluded from the grievance and arbitration procedure, (5) the contract is deemed to be cancelled on particular types of contract violations; (6) noncompliance with decisions and awards is charged, or (7) the grievance machinery breaks down. (49)

As a process that typically precedes arbitration, the grievance procedure contains several ingredients that have the potential for contaminating the merits of the case if and when it eventually arrives at an arbitration proceeding. The most prominent and frequently occurring of such ingredients are reviewed here, with examples given of relevant cases: (1) what constitutes a grievance, (2) what constitutes sufficiency in a grievance, (3) the differences between an individual and the union filing a grievance, (4) the effect of time limits on filing, (5) the effect of time limits on grievance steps during processing, (6) the pertinence of the date of occurrence or the grievance, (7) the effect of the absence of specified time limits, and (8) the filing of grievances by the employer.

In broad outline, grievances procedures follow a relatively standardized pattern, while wide variations show up in the details. In agreements for large companies and large multiemployer situations, the formalization of the grievance process is necessarily extended beyond the degree appropriate for smaller establishments. As a whole, agreements for large undertakings tend to be more complicated; large companies need more rules and more formality in these rules than do small companies; and there are more levels of authority at which the final satisfactory settlement may be sought in large companies and associations and in the unions with which they bargain. In general, the grievance machinery is set up as a succession of steps through which complaints may be processed from lower to higher management and union ranks, and ultimately to arbitration if the parties are unable to resolve their differences themselves.

Variations in procedure usually concern the manner in which grievances are initiated, the number of steps, time limits, writing requirements, compensation for employees involved in the handling of grievances as union representatives, and the details of arbitration. Differences also exist in the issues subject to the grievance procedure. In recent years, for example, some contracts have required that complaints arising out of the administration of insurance and pension plans be processed separately from the usual grievance procedure because of their complexity.

The grievance machinery analyzed in the previously cited study (49) showed that procedures ranged from a single informal type to highly formalized series of six steps or more; but the overwhelming majority of contracts specified three or four steps.

For these reasons, grievance provisions themselves are not subject to precise analysis and are not reported here in any detail. However, it is possible to consider the eight basic areas previously mentioned, from the point of view of certain established labor-relations concepts, as they have evolved from arbitral judgments over the years.

WHAT CONSTITUTES A GRIEVANCE?

What is a grievance? Is it any dispute between the parties? Is it any complaint or problem raised by an employee? The definitions of grievance found in thousands of labor agreements have numerous variations. Typical of a broad and loosely worked provision is one that would read: "Any dispute, disagreement, or difference arising between any employee or the union and the company may be presented as a grievance."

Such an umbrella clause is generally sought by the union, for it would probably allow the union or an employee to raise any conceivable type of claim or complaint, with or without contractual coverage, and be entitled to a labor-management hearing, perhaps up to and including arbitration. In the absence of any other regulatory clause in the grievance and arbitration provision, an arbiter might be free to decide the claim on its face. Naturally, the potential dangers intrinsic to, if not in fact invited by such a broad definition, are quite intimidating to many employers. "Any dispute" could embrace the size of the food portions in the caterer's food-dispensing machines. "Any disagreement" might include the foreman's failure to invite an employee to a private party held in his own home. And would probably include almost every other imaginable kind of complaint on the part of the employee or union. Lest they be dismissed as tilting at windmills, these examples are not hypothetical; they have been experienced by employers under this kind of contractual language.

This is one of the reasons why employers try to shy away from such all-inclusive definitions. There are others, and these turn primarily on the concept of management rights.

Most of today's employers view the labor agreement as the sole and complete embodiment of the mutual commitments between management and labor for the duration of its term, and as including all of the mutual promises and restrictions. Therefore, since the agreement presumably holds all of the limitations, restrictions, prohibitions, and regulatory controls on management actions, management typically lays claim to all remaining managerial prerogatives. These are commonly referred to in labor-relations circles as residual, reserved, or inherent rights. Fortunately for employers, the vast majority of arbitrators subscribe to the concept and theory of management's "residual" rights, namely, that, unless the company's ability to act or decide has been proscribed by some controlling contractual provision, management retains the right to exercise its own discretion and judgment over any matter.

In general, bargaining consists of an attempt by the union to persuade the company to accept limitations upon the exercise of certain previously unrestricted managerial rights. In principle, what this means is that the parties have written a contract as an instrument containing specific and limited restrictions on the functions that management would otherwise be free to exercise if a union were not on the premises.

In light of these concepts, it is perhaps predictable that employers prefer a much narrower and more confining definition of "grievance." They do not wish to allow the union to use the grievance and arbitration provisions as a means of engaging in "fishing expeditions" to obtain concessions not yet granted. Nor do they want the grievance procedure to be used to further erode what freedom they have left after bargaining.

For these reasons, the most frequently encountered definition of grievance is more specific. It uses such terms as "interpretation," "application," "compliance," either singularly or in combination, to describe what would constitute a grievance, subject to the procedures established.

Most often the definition of grievance is worded somewhat along the following lines: "In the event that any difference arises between the company and the Union, or any employee, concerning the interpretation, application, or compliance with the provisions of this agreement, such difference shall be deemed to be a grievance and shall be settled only in accordance with the grievance procedure set forth herein." (50) Accordingly, such a provision imposes two yardsticks by which the validity of a given complaint must be measured to determine if it meets the test of being "deemed to be a grievance." First, the dispute must concern the provisions of the agreement; second, having met that condition, it must subsequently retain its meritorious standing by being "settled only in accordance with the grievance procedure set forth" in the contract.

In administering the contract, the course followed by the majority of managements in connection with any grievance is to seek the answers to two basic questions from the union: (1) What provision is allegedly violated? and (2) How did the company violate this provision? This strategy holds several definite advantages.

- It tends to contain the grievance arguments within the terms and conditions of the labor agreement.
- It tends to provide a disciplining factor by furthering the objective of maintaining a businesslike atmosphere in the grievance meeting.
- During the course of the grievance discussion, if the union is unable to produce sound and viable arguments and facts to support its contentions about "what" and "how," such failure may enlighten and discourage them from processing claims lacking merit.
- It provides both parties with insights into the validty of their respective positions, their strengths and shortcomings, and enables better preparation and planning for arbitration.

How have arbitrators dealt with the question of what constitutes a grievance? Three examples follow.

At the United States Steel Corporation, a grievance was filed by a union committeeman on behalf of a former employee to recover the employee's accrued vacation pay. It was deemed nonarbitrable by arbitrator Herbert L. Sherman, Jr., who ruled that it did not qualify as a "grievance of an employee," within the meaning of the contract, or as a "union grievance," under a clause providing for the processing of grievances "which allege a violation of the obligations of the Company to the Union as such." (51)

In another instance, the American Body and Equipment Company refused to meet with the union at the third step of the grievance procedure to discuss a union grievance over alleged misconduct of a supervisor. Arbitrator A. Langley Coffee ruled that the agreement had not been violated since, under the contract, discipline of supervisors was a "management function" not subject to the grievance procedure. (52)

In the next example, a different set of circumstances led to a different conclusion. In this case, a retired employee had complained that the employer's action in making her retire involuntarily violated her seniority rights. The company had contended that the administration of its retirement program was within its complete discretion and not subject to the grievance or arbitration provisions of the contract. However, the agreement contained a provision stating that any employee complaint, without exception, about which there was a dispute as to interpretation "which is reduced to writing and delivered by a union representative, within 60 days of the action complained of shall be considered and handled as a formal grievance." Arbitrator James V. Altieri ruled that the employer violated the contract by refusing to submit to the grievance procedure, since the complaint had been reduced to writing and delivered as prescribed within 60 days of the forced retirement. In view of the contract clause, he held that the complaint raised substantial questions concerning the true intent, meaning, and application of the contract and other agreements between the parties. Accordingly, it constituted a grievance within the meaning of the contract provisions. (53)

The arbitral rationale in the three cases illustrated is instructive. In the last instance, the broad and embracing language of the grievance machinery enabled coverage of a dispute dealing with the forced retirement of an individual, calling into play the retirement plan and the seniority provisions. In the first two instances, one constituted a grievance "for" the employee rather than "of" the employee, as contractually required. In the other, a complaint seeking discipline of a supervisor for alleged misconduct could not constitute a legitimate grievance within the terms of the agreement. Although there are many more published examples, these are sufficient to demonstrate arbitral interpretations of what may constitute a grievance.

SUFFICIENCY OF GRIEVANCE

At the Hayes Aircraft Corporation, arbitrator John Ansley Griffin allowed the union to get by without specifying in the blanks provided on the printed grievance form the contract sections relating to the discharge procedure. The union's failure to provide such information on the form itself did not constitute an improper filing, or a defective grievance by reason of insufficiency, because its position had been set out fully in a statement attached to the grievance form. The company's objection to the insufficiency of the grievance was viewed merely as technical nit-picking. The arbitrator chose to view the grievance as a whole, rather than as two separate and unrelated documents. (54)

Needless to say, the above-mentioned contract did oblige the union to specify the sections of the agreement relating to the dispute. Therefore, under certain circumstances, the absence of such identification could produce a defective grievance instrument. However, in a case involving the Sinclair Refining Company, in which the contract did not explicitly require citation of specific provisions, arbitrator James J. Willingham held that the fact that the written grievance did not cite the contractual provision allegedly violated did not bar arbitration of the grievance. (55)

There can be other influencing factors that make an apparently incomplete grievance sufficient on its face to merit arbitral review. Some of these came into play in a case involving Black, Sivoils, and Bryson, Inc., and arbitrated by Byron Abernathy. Here, although the union's grievance failed to indicate with much clarity the nature of the grievance, the grievance was nonetheless deemed arbitrable because (1) the employer had failed to object that the grievance was improperly written until it reached the arbitration step of the procedure, (2) the grievance cited the specific provision of the contract, and, (3) although protesting about the vagueness of the grievance statement, the employer was not, in fact, in the dark or uninformed about the nature of the grievance at the time it came to arbitration. (56)

The next two cases are outstanding examples of disputes in which arbitrators found that the grievances contained fatal inadequacies. In the first, a grievance seeking back pay had been signed by one grievant, but contained the phrase "approximately 10 or more men involved." The arbitrator upheld the grievance, but did not grant the unnamed but similarly situated employees the benefits of the back-pay award on the premises that (1) "10 or more men" who failed to sign the grievance also failed thereby to establish "the fact that they had a difference of opinion with the employer" on the matter; (2) the union failed to prove that other employees had a legitimate grievance of a similar nature when it failed to supply the names of the employees, as requested by the company; and (3) the other employees forfeited their rights, if any, to have the grievance adjusted because they had not established the fact that they were grievants within the three-day contractual time limit for filing grievances. The failure of the employees to identify themselves with the grievance was wrong because (1) it is unfair to expect one employee to carry the fight for the others who remained anonymous in the background, (2) the employer was unable to evaluate the grievance with a view to a possible compromise without knowledge of the employees involved, and (3) the grievance procedure was not intended to permit one party to withhold important facts of the dispute. So ruled arbitrator Raphael Morvant at the Geigy Chemical Corporation. (57)

In a case at the Magnavox Company, the union's grievance had demanded "satisfactory job descriptions" pursuant to National Labor Relations Board (NLRB) order and the terms of the collective bargaining contract. Arbitrator Harry Dworkin said the grievance was too general and vague to be arbitrable, since it constituted, in effect, a general complaint that job descriptions furnished by the employer were not satisfactory, without specifying contract clauses involved, individual descriptions complained of, or discrepancies alleged to exist between the write-up and the job performance. Second, the relief sought was an order directing the employer to negotiate with the union on proper job descriptions, notwithstanding the fact that neither the NLRB order nor the contract obligated the company to do so. Accordingly, Dworkin decided that he lacked the authority to compel the parties to engage in a collective bargaining process in the form and manner requested and that the question of compliance with the NLRB order was only within the province of that agency. (58)

Presuming the grievance meets all time-limit requirements of the contract, if any, other contractual provisions may impose additional substantive or procedural requirements. Some examples have already been given, but there can be others. For instance, does the contractual grievance procedure require that an employee grievant be signatory to the grievance? Does the contract require an oral discussion among the employee, the foremen, and the union representative prior to the writing of the grievance? It is always desirable and advisable to examine the written grievance for any such defects. If a shortcoming in the instrument is discovered, one should consider the possible effect of that defect on one's ability to deal reasonably with and to dispose of the issue raised. If some contractual requirement is not met because of an omission or a defect in the grievance, it should be called to the other party's attention as soon as it is discovered. The failure to do so at the earliest practicable time may result in forfeiture of a subsequent valid opportunity to contest the issue through the grievance process. If the omission or defect results in an impairment of its ability to comprehend or resolve the matter a party may legitimately ask the other party to remove or clarify the inadequacy.

INDIVIDUAL VERSUS UNION FILING OF GRIEVANCE

The National Labor Relations Act (NLRA) requires employers to bargain with the representative selected by the majority of the employees in the appropriate unit as "the exclusive representative of all the employees in such unit for the purpose of collective bargaining." Section 9(a) of the NLRA was amended in 1947 to read as follows: "Any individual employee or group of employees shall have the right at any time to present grievances to their employer and to have such grievances adjusted without the intervention of the bargaining representative, as long as the adjustment is not inconsistent with the terms of the collective bargaining contract or agreement that is in effect; provided further, that the bargaining representative has been given opportunity to be present at such adjustment." It has been held that this proviso grants individual employees the right to process their own grievances. (59) Clearly, this proviso enabling an individual employee to present and argue his own personal case with management does not stretch so far as to allow grievance settlements that are not in accord with the terms and conditions of the existing labor contract.

This statutory condition, however, does not preclude the parties from agreeing to other contractual conditions with regard to the techniques and mechanics of grievance processing, which may affect the validity and merits of a given dispute before an arbitrator. For example, under the grievance procedure of a contract that referred to the "affected employee" and required that a grievance be "signed by the employee," it was held by arbitrator Walter Seinsheimer that the union did not have the right to file a policy grievance. However, he concluded that this should not limit the union in policing the contract, since in his view all provisions in one way or another affected an employee or employees. In this case, in which vacation pay was sought for a discharged employee, he said that the grievance should have been signed by the discharged employee. (60) The union's grievance about policy, therefore, was invalid.

Where the wording of the contract is more permissive and less compelling than in the foregoing example, a different result may follow. In a case in which the contract required only that "if the question is not then settled, the employee may submit his grievance in writing," arbitrator James Willingham ruled that the fact that a written grievance was signed by a union representative and not by the grievant did not bar arbitration of it on its merits. Also relevant to the validity of the grievance was the fact that the grievant here knowingly permitted processing of this claim. (61) It is interesting that the employee's giving the union permission to process the dispute affecting him was considered pertinent.

At the Whiteway Stamping Company, arbitrator Samuel Kates was dealing with a different regulatory provision. There, it was decided that the union might process through arbitration a grievance concerning alleged errors in a seniority list, although two employees who signed the grievance wished to withdraw the claim. Arbitrator Kates considered it pertinent that the relative seniority of any employee is ordinarily of concern to all union employees and the evidence did not indicate that the alleged error would not affect employees other than those signing the grievance. Additionally, the union committee also signed the grievance. Contractual provisions did not preclude that body from joining in the action. (62)

A final example demonstrates somewhat the impact that prior practices between the parties may have on current situations. John Day Larkin sat as the neutral third party in a dispute at the Berg Airlectro Products Company. (63) He deemed arbitrable grievances protesting the discharges of the union's president and treasurer, although they had not been signed by the discharged employees but by the chairman of the union grievance committee. The practice of a former personnel director had been to accept written grievances signed by the chairman of the union's grievance committee. He had not insisted upon the signature of an actual aggrieved employee. Furthermore, the employer, by taking the discharge action at a meeting with the union counsel and its international representative, waived at least some of the earlier grievance steps. Furthermore, the employer was advised by the union at that very time that the matter would definitely be brought to arbitration.

In a later chapter, the weight accorded to past practices by arbitrators will be given more coverage. Needless to say, this is one of the more uncertain areas dealt with by practitioners in the labor-management community. (64)

SPECIFIED TIME LIMITS ON FILING

Many labor agreements contain provisions within the grievance procedure which require the union or the employee to file grievances within specified time periods and to process and appeal them from step to step within certain time limitations. Some agreements even impose penalties, such as deeming the grievance settled on the basis of the company's last answer when the employee or the union has not complied. Many such contracts also contain time limits on management, usually for providing an answer to the grievance or scheduling a meeting within the procedure. Such time limits are placed in labor agreements to provide employees with prompt and expeditious handling of their problems.

The observance of contractual time limits in the handling of labor grievances is a two-way street. Management should not insist upon strict compliance by the employees and the union and, at the same time, neglect its own contractual obligations to provide expeditious processing of disputes.

Frequently, labor agreements provide that if the company does not answer in the prescribed time the union may appeal the grievance to the next step of the procedure. The failure of management to answer within the time allowed is generally not interpreted as an admission of default in the grievance, since the burden of moving the complaint to the next step rests with the union and the grievant—not with management. (65)

Less frequently encountered are grievance clauses that consider complaints settled in line with the demand of the grievance when management defaults in observing the prescribed time limits. (66) On the other hand, if both parties have been guilty of contract violations within the grievance procedure, the time limitations will usually not be enforced by arbitrators. (67)

Before discussing certain representative arbitral conclusions, we shall examine a provision that typically closes the grievance procedure and precedes the arbitration clause in the contract. The following is an example of the type most often sought by management's bargaining representatives:

> The parties agree to follow the foregoing Grievance Procedure in accordance with the steps, time limits and conditions contained therein. If, in any step, the Company's representative fails to give his written answer within the time limit therein set forth, the Union may appeal the grievance to the next step at the expiration of such time limit. If the employee or the Union fails to follow the foregoing procedure in accordance with the steps, time limits and conditions therein set forth, the grievance shall be deemed settled on the basis of the Company's last answer. (68)

The penalties for default here appear to be unusual, but they are not. It must be remembered that the union is the moving party on grievances. Therefore, it may choose to allow the grievance to die by merely neglecting to move it from one step to another. Its failure to pursue it may understandably be interpreted as such as a choice. However, management's failure to answer cannot be interpreted as agreement with the grievance claim. It is merely due to procrastination or inadvertence, which should not be allowed to delay the process.

The ways in which time limits have been evaluated by arbitrators makes a fascinating study, and it discloses a definite and logical pattern. As a first example, a contract at Geigy Chemical Corporation contained two relevant conditions. It required that grievances be processed one at a time, and stated that no grievance would be accepted unless it had been presented in the first step within three days of the occurrence of the "incident first giving rise to same." The union's grievance here claimed violation of a contract provision barring discriminatory treatment of employees. The case was based on incidents involving the same employee, which had occurred over a period of nearly one month and concerning which grievances had been filed and either abandoned or withdrawn. The instant grievance was deemed nonarbitrable. It was held to be untimely with regard to the early incidents, and an attempt to combine in one case a number of distinct incidents that should have been processed as separate complaints. However, incidents that had occurred three days prior to the filing of the grievance, and which resulted from a single act of the employee, were within contractual time limits and properly constituted a single grievance. (69)

A somewhat similar decision was handed down by arbitrator Frank Uible at the Sheller Manufacturing Corporation. The contract required that a grievance be filed within 10 working days of the date on which the aggrieved employees had knowledge of the facts giving rise to the grievance. The union's grievance protesting a series of subcontracting incidents was deemed timely only with regard to the incidents occurring within the 10-working-day limit. (70)

It has already been mentioned that even clearly defined time limits may be compromised, as exemplified in the following incident. A grievance filed four days after the discharge of an employee was ruled arbitrable, even though the contract clearly specified that a grievance had to be filed within three days of the occurrence. Why? Because two of the four intervening days were Christmas and Sunday, and, further, the employer made no objection to such delay until the arbitration proceeding. (71) The outcome was predictable.

Under an agreement at the Kaiser Aluminum and Chemical Corporation, grievances were to be filed within 30 days of the occurrence giving rise to the dispute. Seniority grievances filed more than two years after the occasions on which the grievants claimed they should have been assigned to higher-rated jobs on a new machine were called nonarbitrable by Whitley McCoy. (72) Again, because of fatal default in timely filing and processing, the merits of the alleged claim were never considered.

The following case provides another example of how definite time limits may be widened by management's own doing. Under a contract stating that grievances protesting discharges must be filed in writing within three days of the action, a discharge protest filed eight days after the action was held to be arbitrable. What factors produced this finding? First, the employer was informed orally that the union challenged the discharge. Second, the delay in filing a written grievance was occasioned, at least in part, by a mutual agreement to reinstate the employee if he passed a lie-detector test, which he subsequently refused to take. Therefore, for some period of time after the limited discharge action, the certainty and finality of the employer's decision remained in question. (73)

Among the conclusions to be drawn from this study are the following:

- If one party has not met the time limits, the arbitrator is likely to uphold the position of the other if its position is clearly presented and supported by the facts.
- Loose prior administration in handling of contractual time limitations may jeopardize a present case.
- If the wording or the agreement is vague, it may not be clearly and tightly interpreted by the arbitrator.
- If the company has been guilty of looseness in meeting its own contractual time limits, it is doubtful that an arbitrator will tightly enforce those required of the union.
- If the company is guilty of some action or inaction that contributes to the union's untimely filing of a grievance, the arbitrator will not penalize the union.

When handling grievances that appear to be procedurally irregular in the time-limit area, it should be realized that some violations may be of a "continuing" nature. One highly respected authority states: "Numerous arbitrators have held that 'continuing' violations of the Agreement (as opposed to a single, isolated and completed transaction) give rise to 'continuing' grievances in the sense that the act complained of may be said to be repeated from day to day—each day there is a new 'occurrence'; these arbitrators have permitted the filing of such grievances at any time, this not being deemed a violation of the specific time limits stated in the Agreement (although any back pay ordinarily runs only from the date of filing)" (74) An example of a "continuing violation" would be a case in which the company was erroneously paying an individual employee less than the prescribed contractual wage. Every day this shortage occurred would constitute a violation that would start a new time period within which a grievance could be filed.

Clearly, one of the purposes of time-limit provisions in a grievance procedure is to prevent the filing of stale grievances about incidents that occurred only once, at a specific time and place—for example, a warning given to an employee for leaving his work area without permission. It is generally clear that parties do not want protests of this kind presented weeks or months after the incident occurred.

It is also equally clear that neither party wants the other to engage in a *continuing* violation of the terms or the contract and get off scot-free if, for one reason or another, a grievance is not filed within the prescribed time limit following the first occurrence. If such an interpretation were permitted, it could encourage violations of the contract when this might be to the advantage of one side or the other. The rule would then be, if you do not get caught in the first *x* number of days, you may continue the violation with impunity. (75)

TIME LIMITS ON GRIEVANCE STEPS

More than 9 out of every 10 labor agreements define the steps to be followed in processing and adjusting grievances. Three-step procedures (not including arbitration) are by far the most prevalent, appearing in almost 40 percent of all labor agreements. The next most common are the four-step procedures, which appear in approximately 30 percent of contracts. Three-step procedures seem to be the rule in chemicals, fabricated metals, nonelectrical machinery, textiles, transportation equipment, and transportation. Four-step procedures are found most frequently in electrical machinery, paper, primary metals, rubber, communications, and utilities. Two-step procedures are fairly common in food, and outnumber all other arrangements in construction.

Although grievances must be initiated within a stated period in '81 percent of labor contracts (88 percent in manufacturing, 60 percent in nonmanufacturing), time limits applicable to later steps of the grievance procedure are written into only 53 percent of the contracts (61 percent in manufacturing, 29 percent in nonmanufacturing). (76) However, these time limitations are just as important and binding as those applicable to the initial filing of the matter. A review of arbitration awards shows that arbitrators expect the parties to observe the procedural time-limit requirements as a "condition precedent" to their assumption of jurisdiction over the case. Time limits bind the parties as they do the arbitrator.

It is a generally accepted principle of contract law that if both parties grow lax in complying with a provision imposing a time element, the party that first seeks to return to the strict observance must issue a warning to that effect. It has been stated as follows: "The rule is especially applicable where there has been a waiver of the time stipulation in a contract. Time cannot again be made of the essence without notice to the party in default requiring performance within a reasonable time to be specified in the notice and stating that if there is not performance within this time the contract will be abrogated, or without conduct equivalent to notice." Virtually every jurisdiction has its decisions supporting this view, but in *Crocker Chair Company* v. *Edward Hines Hardwood and Hemlock Company* the Wisconsin Supreme Court gave typical expression to it by holding that before one party could impose a default upon the other because it had failed to meet a deadline theretofore largely ignored by the parties, it was necessary to give warning that such course of conduct no longer would be tolerated and that the terms of the contract thenceforth would be enforced. (77)

If the company itself is lax over a period of time in observing time limitations, it may act to erode and reduce the binding effectiveness of the provisions of the contract. The following are examples of the most commonly negotiated arrangements for applying time limitations on grievance processing. One states: "Failure of any party to abide by the time limits set forth in this procedure shall make the position of the last party abiding by these limits final and binding upon all parties" (78) Plainly, in this instance, the parties intended a similar penalty to be imposed upon each other for any defaults. The other arrangement is usually more desirable from the employer's viewpoint: "Failure of the employee or the guild to proceed within any time limit set forth in the procedure hereinabove stated shall constitute a waiver of the grievance, unless such time limit has been extended by the written consent of the company and the guild. Failure of the company to act within the time limits set forth in any step shall entitle the guild to proceed to the next step." (79)

How are provisions such as these interpreted or enforced in arbitration? One contract provided that a grievance that was "not referred or appealed to the next step within specified time limits" was considered settled on the basis of the company's previous answer. The grievance of a laid-off union steward was not processed to the third step of the grievance procedure within the two-day limit of the second step. It was ruled not to have been processed within the terms of the agreement; therefore, arbitrator Harry Dworkin declined to consider the merits of the grievance.

The practice of these parties, had been that in grievances concerning union stewards the first step of the procedure was bypassed and they were processed initially in the second step. Thus, the parties' first meeting was actually a "second step," and at that time the employer answered the complaint by affirming the propriety of its previous layoff action. The steward took no further action with respect to his grievance until four working days after the meeting. He was two days too late. (80)

What happens when the contract does not specify the penalty for defaulting on time limitations? Arbitrator Frank Elkouri answered that question in his decision on the following case.

In this instance, the labor agreement stated that the employer's answer would be given within 10 days from the date the grievance was appealed to Step 4; further, the grievance might be appealed to arbitration within 10 days from receipt of the answer or be considered settled and not subject to arbitration. It was held that a grievance might be appealed to arbitration without further delay if the employer had not filed his answer within 10 days from the date of appeal to Step 4. On the other hand, if the answer was given within the contractual 10-day period, the union was entitled to appeal it to arbitration within 10 working days from receipt of such answer. (81)

Another dispute, with still other quirks and turns, produced typical arbitral rationale: The contract stated that the employer would "answer grievances within 10 days after the presentation or referral to Step 4"; further, if such grievances were not answered within the specified time limits, they would be considered granted. Clearly, the burden on the employer was great. The question that came up was how closely such time limits were to be counted from beginning to closing. The employer had mailed answers to 23 job-classification grievances at 11:50 A.M. on the day on which the union claimed the 10-day period expired at 8:30 A.M. Fortunately for the company, arbitrator Paul Lehoczky did not agree. He found that the parties had never before interpreted the grievance-procedure time limits on a "minute and hour" basis, and to him it was inconceivable that the employer, under these circumstances and aware of the forfeiture clause of the contract, would have permitted grievances of this consequence to be granted by default. (82)

The last case to be cited here deals with still another issue: A grievance protesting the discharge of an employee was deemed arbitrable even though the union did not comply with the time limits for processing grievances as set out in the contract. Further, the agreement specifically stated that exceptions to the time limits might be made by mutual agreement, but such agreements had to be in writing to be considered valid. No such extension had been agreed upon. Why, then, was the union upheld in spite of its procedural default? The arbitrator discovered that neither the employer nor the union had regularly abided by time limits or followed the prescribed steps in the procedure. While there was no agreement in writing constituting a mutual waiver, arbitrator Walter Seinsheimer felt that the parties had, in actuality, agreed "to violate the specified time limits" by their actions and behavior in disregarding them. (83)

DATE OF OCCURRENCE OR EMPLOYEE'S KNOWLEDGE

Typical grievance-procedure clauses provide that the grievance is to be filed and time limits are to commence from the date of "the occurrence or its discovery." Naturally, not every grievance is discovered at the time the contested action occurs. Such issues often cause consternation among arbitrators; most frequently, however, they decide that a grievant cannot be expected to file a grievance until he is, or should have been, aware of the event upon which he claims a violation. (84)

One of the first questions is, What constitutes an "occurrence"? Arbitrator Samuel Ladar gave his opinion in a case involving the American Pipe and Construction Company. He held that the company did not fail to abide by the grievance procedure, or violate the labor agreement, when it went ahead with plans to perform work in a manner alleged by the union to contravene the contract. The company's mere intention or threat to engage in such a course of conduct, as it had announced, did not constitute a grievance in the eyes of this neutral. A bona fide grievance first required an actual occurrence. The basis for a grievance could exist only after the company went ahead with its plans. (85)

It is interesting to note a comparison. In the above-cited case, the employer contended no valid grievance could arise until the date of the actual action. In the next case, the employer complained that a time limit for filing a grievance was in effect from the date he announced an intended future action. However, the arbitrator in this situation followed the same logic as Ladar. The contract here required the filing of grievances within five days of the "incident" complained of. A grievance protesting removal of a machine to another plant for repairs filed within five days of the date on which the machine was removed was held to meet the time requirements, although the union had been advised of the employer's decision to take this action on an earlier data. (86)

The same arbitral logic was pursued in another instance, although the factual situation gave rise to an interesting and different problem: The labor agreement provided that the grievance was to be presented "within three days of the alleged incident or cause." A grievance filed ten days after the employer had noted "no successful bidder" on a posted notice of a job vacancy protested the employer's refusal to award the job to the grievant. Deemed untimely, the claim was dismissed despite the fact that the grievance was filed within three days of the actual filling of the vacancy. Why? The arbitrator reasoned that the notation on the posted vacancy constituted a clear and unequivocal rejection of the employee's bid for the job. Such notice did not constitute an announcement of a future company action; it was an action in and of itself. (87)

NO TIME LIMIT SPECIFIED IN CONTRACT

Some contracts contain no specific time limits for instituting grievances; instead, they impose the general requirement that "grievances must be filed with reasonable promptness." The lack of definite time limits for initial presentation as well as for processing of grievances can create difficulties for both union and employer. Time limits should not be considered a substitute for good faith in the grievance procedure; the two factors do not conflict. A time limitation merely ensures that a complaint will get a prompt and fresh hearing and move expeditiously to an early conclusion. Undue delay at any stage of the procedure can render the process meaningless or ineffective. Failure to impose time limits on appeals may also allow the revival of long-dead complaints or of grievances so old that the relevant facts cannot be reconstructed.

In most cases in which there were no specific time limits, arbitrators have generally held that grievances must be filed promptly, unless justifiably delayed. (88) However, the interpretation of "prompt filing" by one arbitrator may be quite different from that of another.

Arbitrator Peter Kelliher in a Creamery Package Manufacturing case ruled that filing of a layoff grievance three weeks after the employee was laid off was not "prompt" within the meaning of the contract. (89)

Arbitrator Ralph Seward in a National Tube Company case ruled that a 10-month delay in filing a grievance did not bar consideration of its merits when management had deliberately withheld pertinent information from the union. (90)

Under the contract of the New York Racing Association, the parties had agreed "to meet promptly through authorized representatives, after notification by either party, to discuss and adjust grievances." In interpreting this provision, an arbiter concluded he could not consider the merits of a grievance filed in April 1963 protesting the company's failure to rehire an employee when the employer's first refusal to rehire him occurred in March 1961. While the agreement did not specify a time period for the filing of a dispute, that such complaints should be filed within a reasonable time was implicit. The opinion of the neutral third party was that such a requirement was particularly clear in situations such as that one, where the grievant had to be held responsible for the delay because he had refused to file a grievance sooner. (91)

At the American Bakeries Company, the union held a grievance in abeyance, pending occurrence of a similar incident. Under a contract which did not explicitly authorize such withholding but in which there were no contractual time limits for the processing of grievances, the issue was held to be arbitrable. (92)

It can be seen, then, that any number of potential problems may result when a contract does not specify time limits for filing and processing grievances. An arbitrator cannot consult a crystal ball during such disputes to find out what the parties had in mind and what they considered "reasonably prompt" at the time the contract was drawn up. Even if he could, it is doubtful that any clear picture would emerge. What may be construed as "reasonably prompt" by one party may be quite different in the eyes of the other. It may be for that very reason that the parties have inserted such wording in their agreement, making it susceptible to more than one interpretation. This is often the result when each party is seeking a different bargaining objective and neither is willing to compromise sufficiently to reach a specifically worded understanding. By consenting to such wording as "reasonably prompt," they are disposing of their *instant* difference of opinion—though often only temporarily. In so doing, both save face and arrive at an agreement without a strike impasse. However, the impasse is merely postponed. Eventually, they must relate the term "reasonably prompt" to a particular grievance and try to agree on an applicable time period. Then an arbitrator must be called to define the term for them. The end result is the handing down of his opinion as to what time period is within, or without, the intended confines of "reasonably prompt."

The negotiation of penalties for failure to observe a standard of promptness is a natural outgrowth of such procedures, for without penalties the integrity of timely processing may easily be destroyed. Even where there's no time, and even in the absence of a "settlement penalty" against the company for its untimely handling of a complaint, every effort should be made to deal with the matter in a very prompt manner, without delay or hesitation. The union usually goes after tight time limitations on management's grievance handling—and justifiably—when management's representatives have been inattentive or negligent in their obligation to meet promptly, discuss promptly, and answer promptly the employees' grievances. Management has an interest in preventing grievances from festering, wasting, and souring. Employees have the right to expect and receive prompt and expeditious treatment of their problems.

EMPLOYER GRIEVANCES

The Bureau of National Affairs (BNA) has reported that just under one sixth of all contracts specify management's right to have access to the grievance machinery. This right is available in nearly 16 percent of manufacturing agreements and 14 percent of non-manufacturing contracts. Provisions of this nature appear in at least one fifth of the agreements in the following industries: apparel, chemicals, construction, insurance and finance, leather, machinery, shipping, petroleum, transportation equipment, and utilities. (93)

An example of a clause that enables management to initiate grievances is the following: "Any grievance which the Company

may have against the Union shall be reduced to writing and submitted to the shop chairman who will promptly arrange a meeting
at the third stage of the grievance procedure. If the matter is not
satisfactorily settled at this meeting, or within five (5) days thereafter, the grievance may be processed through Steps 4 and 5 of
the grievance procedure." (94) While this clause allows management to introduce written grievances into the parties' procedures,
it is, nevertheless, silent on the question of what would happen
to any unresolved dispute. Could the employer then move the
issue along into an arbitral proceeding? Or does the absence of
explicit language in this connection suggest that it was not intended by the parties that management could demand and compel
arbitration once it had exhausted the internal machinery of the
dispute processes?

Such doubt is removed in the next example, in which the clause
certainly leaves no doubt about the employer's opportunity to
obtain arbitration for any unresolved complaints: "The company
may present any dispute arising under, or matters of interpretation
of, this agreement or any grievance against the union direct to the
labor relations board with the right to arbitration under section
. . . hereof."

How have arbitrators interpreted and applied such provisions?

Under a contract stating that it provided for "the orderly and
amicable settlement of any and all disputes, differences, and grievances arising out of the meaning or application of the terms of this
agreement," arbitrator Frank Elkouri ruled that the employer had
the right to submit grievances, there being no other contractual
provision that denied such a right. (95)

Arbitrator Clair Duff, concerning a contract at the Schofield
Manufacturing Company, held that the employer had the right to
submit grievances to arbitration even though the agreement was
silent on the subject. The decision was based on the premise that
the employer had renounced his right to use of a lockout by expressed language, and that it would be unfair to decide that the
company possessed the right to neither grievance nor to lockout.
Duff believed that had the parties wished to burden their contract
with such a disadvantage, it would have been stated specifically.
(96)

A district court in Connecticut once held that both the employer, the Federal Paper Board Company, and the union, Paper-

makers and Paperworkers, could submit to arbitration a dispute over the union's alleged breach of a no-strike article. Their agreement contained a clause stating that "either party to the dispute" might submit a matter to arbitration. No language in the contract expressly or implicitly limited the employer's right to do so. (97)

It has been seen that some labor agreements leave avenues open for management to file grievances and seek and obtain arbitration for final redress. But is it either desirable or advisable to do so? That raises a wholly different kind of question. According to one school of thought, initiation of grievances on the part of management, should be a rarely used and carefully considered action.

The typical labor agreement contains some type of no-strike pledge by the union, usually coupled with the employer's promise that he will not lock out employees during the term of the contract. (98) Such a no-strike promise is one of the few useful concessions made to the company by the union. With the exception of the no-strike pledge, all other provisions of the agreement generally constitute a limitation on, or prohibition or compromise of, management rights. Thus, following the residual theory of management rights, an employer should accord with the posture that "management acts—the union reacts." As a "defense" organization, the union reacts to management-initiated decisions and actions by filing a grievance in protest. The only aggressive act in which the union can engage, thus causing management to "react," is conduct violating the no-strike pledge. Among the few issues over which management might consider filing its own grievance, the union's violation of the no-strike promise would be number one.

Apart from such theoretical considerations, what effect, if any, does the use of the grievance procedure against a no-strike violation have on the ability or right of management to seek other judicial relief? Naturally, the assumption made here is that the labor agreement permits (or does not expressly preclude) the company's use of the grievance and arbitration processes. The advisability of having a contract in which management may resort to the grievance procedure is doubtful, at best, in the view of many management adherents, including this author. What is of concern is the possible detrimental effect such a provision would have on the company's ability to obtain fuller and more complete relief—injunction or compensatory or punitive damages—in the courts, rather than before an arbitrator. This must be viewed as a valid consideration in the face of the treatment of this issue by the courts.

In a 1962 case, the United States Supreme Court ruled that a company's lawsuit seeking damages caused by a union's alleged violation of a no-strike provision was to be stayed pending an arbitration hearing on the claim. The contractual grievance machinery was sufficiently broad to cover the issue, and the parties, by having made those provisions, had arranged for all disputes to be settled within those processes. By the Court's reasoning, this effectively precluded the company from pursuing its claim through litigation. (99)

In another case on the same day, the Supreme Court upheld the ruling of a lower court denying a union's motion for a stay of the employer's damage suit, which was correct in view of a contractual grievance procedure allowing only the employee or his union to raise and process claims. This contingency thus enabled the company to pursue its damage claim in the courts.

The reasons behind the preference for pursuing claims in the courts as opposed to the arbitration process are fairly obvious. The threat of a large money judgment claimed through the courts must be viewed as a vastly superior deterrent to the union than a claim pursued via the grievance and arbitration routes. Courts do not feel the pressures upon arbitrators to maintain reputations acceptable to both parties. On the whole, considering all factors, courts would be more likely to award a fuller measure of damages. Comparison between recorded court-awarded judgments and those resulting from arbitration decisions reveals that small indeed is the number of arbitration cases that have made awards to management for damages. Whether this stems from a small number of cases being heard or from a small number being published, the conclusion does not favor arbitration. If the former is true, the company is making its claim in an arena where there is a lack of experience; if the latter is true, it probably results from the arbitrators' unwillingness to publicize this issue. In either instance, these are sufficient reasons for management to prefer the judicial route.

Two cases bear review. Courts have held on a number of occasions, and in a number of jurisdictions, that a union was entitled to a stay, pending arbitration of the employer's action under section 301 of the Labor Management Relations Act for damages over a strike in violation of the contract. This was the holding in the light of contracts that did not exclude the question of damages in the arbitration clause. (100) In at least one case, the fact that the employer's plant had been closed since shortly after the termination of the strike and the contract had expired did not bar resort to arbitration. (101)

Finally, in a case in which the contract authorized either party to submit to arbitration any difference arising about the meaning of the enforcement of the contract, the court held that the question of whether the union breached the no-strike article raised an arbitrable issue. More significantly, the employees' failure to comply with the arbitration clause provided the company a complete defense in its action to recover damages from the union because of the episode. (102)

Most managements wisely do not precipitously file grievances or demand arbitration for their problems. If the relevant contract provisions are unclear, ambiguous, or susceptible to more than one interpretation with regard to the company's grievance rights, such doubts may be resolved in favor of "grievance." If the arbitration clause is applicable to the given dispute or if management's filing of a grievance gives more conclusive meaning to otherwise ambiguous language, arbitration may well be ordered. Again, the Steelworkers Trilogy should be considered; there, Chief Justice Douglas spoke for the majority: "An order to arbitrate the particular grievance should not be denied unless it may be said *with positive assurance* that the arbitration clause is *not susceptible* of an interpretation that covers the asserted dispute. Doubts should be resolved in favor of coverage" (emphasis added).

6

Arbitration versus Mediation

IN ORDER to know what arbitration is, it is essential to understand what mediation or conciliation is, how it functions and operates as compared with arbitration. One authority offers the following definition: "By *mediation* or *conciliation* is usually meant the bringing together of employers and employees for a peaceable settlement of their differences by discussion and negotiation. The mediator, either a private or an official individual or board, makes inquiries without compulsory powers, trying to induce the parties by mutual concessions to effect a settlement." (103)

The idea of having an interested but impartial third party mediate in a labor dispute is quite old. In their *Industrial Democracy*, Sidney and Beatrice Webb, prolific English writers of the early 1900s, stressed the value of an "eminent outsider" acting as a "conciliator." They said: "This work of conciliation is, we believe, destined to play a great and for many years an increasing part in the labor struggles of this country." (104) George Barnett and David McCabe had high praise for mediation when in 1916 they wrote: "As among the three kinds of such agencies (i.e., mediation, investigation, and arbitration), it is clear that up to the present by far the best results have been obtained through mediation." (105)

In a more recent report entitled *The Public Interest in National Labor Policy,* a group of scholars concluded, "Government's most effective means of contributing to dispute settlement is to provide mediation services of high quality." (106)

The words "mediation" and "conciliation" are used synonymously by practically all writers in the field. Technically, conciliation simply means bringing the parties together to discuss their dispute. The conciliator has a passive role. In mediation, on the other hand, the mediator has quite an active role. He may act as a go-between and even make suggestions for settling the dispute. (107) This distinction between mediation and conciliation is rarely adhered to, and no lesser authorities than John R. Commons and John B. Andrews use the two words together when explaining the mediation process. (108)

For some 30 years prior to 1913, labor leaders had wanted the federal government to create a department that would represent the interests of the wage earner. There was an attempt to meet this demand when the Department of Commerce and Labor was created on February 14, 1903. (109) This department was to represent the interests of both commerce and labor. The limitations of such a dual obligation are obvious.

On March 4, 1913, Congress established an independent Department of Labor, the purpose of which was to foster, promote, and develop the welfare of the wage earner of the United States, to improve his working conditions, and to advance his opportunities for profitable employment. Although the creation of the new department helped to segregate the affairs of labor from those of management, the Commerce and Labor Act contained a provision that was to prove, at best, bothersome. Section 8 stipulated: "The Secretary of Labor shall have power to act as mediator and to appoint commissioners of conciliation in labor disputes whenever in his judgment the interests of industrial peace may require it to be done." In effect, Congress gave this new department the responsibility of fostering and promoting the welfare of the wage earner while at the same time acting as an impartial mediator in labor disputes. Despite the difficulties of this task, the department received remarkably little complaint of partiality from the business sector.

In its embryonic stage, the Department of Labor considered the mediation function as one of its most important jobs. In his second annual report, the Secretary of Labor said: "Of all the functions of the Department of Labor, which it is yet possible to administer, this one [mediation] may by reasonably regarded as the most important." (110)

The industrial strife of the middle 1930s put an increased load on the department's Conciliation Service. With the coming of the Second World War, industrial activity, which began to increase tremendously, was accompanied by increased labor problems.

By 1941 it was becoming apparent that the United States would be drawn into the war, and interruption of production because of labor disputes was becoming more and more intolerable from the point of view of defense preparations and public opinion. To resolve this, the President, by Executive Order on March 19, 1941, set up the National Defense Mediation Board. The Board was made up of eleven members representing the public, management, and labor. The Board's job was, basically, to try to settle disputes that could not be settled by the commissioners of conciliation in cases in which the defense effort was affected. The Board's recommendations were not binding, according to the Executive Order; in actuality they were, since in three instances decisions of the Board were enforced by the President through seizure of plants. (111) In less than a year, the work of the Board was practically brought to a standstill by the resignation of representatives of the Congress of Industrial Organizations (CIO) from the Board. One of the basic weaknesses of the National Defense Mediation Board was that when its mediation efforts failed and arbitration was refused, the Board was required to make findings and recommendations for settlement. This placed the Board in the position of mediator and quasi-arbitrator. (112) The feeling of most writers in the mediation field is that a mediation service loses its effectiveness when it tries to wear two hats and arbitrate as well as mediate.

MEDIATION AND TAFT-HARTLEY

Many philosophical and ethical questions were raised about the advisability of having a service dedicated to impartiality lodged in the Labor Department, since the purpose of the Labor Department, by law, was "to foster, promote, and develop the welfare of the wage earners of the United States."

During the war, the pendulum of public opinion began to swing away from the labor movement. Labor had been cast in the role of underdog during the 1930s. The strikes and strike threats of the war years convinced the public that Congress had moved too far in the direction of labor. With this mandate from the public, Congress set about to redress the balance of power between labor and management.

The Labor Management Relations Act of 1947 was intended to modify the National Labor Relations Act of 1935. From the discussions prior to its passage, it appears that the proposal to make the conciliation service an independent agency was more or less a rider attached to the bill. Senator Smith, arguing for the move, said the mediation service should be moved outside the Labor Department: "The Department of Labor is by the terms of the statute creating it, and properly so, the advocate of the labor side of controversies. Because of that fact it has been felt that mediation and conciliation should not be left within the Department of Labor, as the wrong atmosphere would surround what is supposed to be an impartial body." (113)

Representative Hartley, from the Committee on Education and Labor, submitted a report saying that the Department of Labor was charged with conflicting duties in trying to represent labor and act as mediator. (114) Senator Taft argued that the Department of Labor had to take a prolabor slant and could not mediate fairly. (115) The main argument in favor of an independent agency, in fact practically the only argument in favor of it, was that, since it was in the Department of Labor, the conciliation service could not be impartial. With the passage of the Taft-Hartley Bill, the present Federal Mediation and Conciliation Service (FMCS) was formed.

Aside from making the new agency independent of the Labor Department, there were some other changes in the character of the Service. The previous United States Conciliation Service (USCS) had had no jurisdictional limitations, whereas the new Service was to be limited to disputes affecting interstate commerce. The act recognized the role of state and other agencies in mediation. It established limitations on the extent to which the Service could intercede in grievance disputes; it also required that parties take part in meetings called by the Service.

Except for a time in World War II, USCS had had no efficient means of learning about disputes and, consequently, often did not know about a dispute until the positions of both sides had been cemented in misunderstanding. To avoid this, the new law made it mandatory for the party seeking to terminate or modify its contract to contact the other party 60 days before the proposed date of change and offer to meet with it to discuss the change. If no agreement was reached within the first 30 days, the parties were required to notify the Service, as well as territorial or state agencies.

MECHANICS OF MEDIATION

After FMCS becomes aware of a dispute, it must decide whether to assign the dispute to a mediator. In making this decision, the Service must be guided by the law, which, however, is open to broad interpretation: "(b) The Service may proffer its services in any labor dispute in any industry affecting commerce, either upon its own motion or upon the request of one or more of the parties to the dispute, whenever in its judgment such dispute threatens to cause a substantial interruption of commerce. The Director and the Service are directed to avoid attempting to mediate disputes which would have only a minor effect on interstate commerce if State or other conciliation services are available to the parties." (116)

In interpreting this provision, it appears that the Service does not consider the determining factor to be the number of persons in the bargaining unit, but rather the effect of the dispute on interstate commerce.

After a mediator has been assigned a dispute case, he will normally contact the company and the union within a short time to ask about the status of their negotiation. If within a week of the deadline nothing has been settled, he may suggest that they all get together, offering but not forcing his service.

What does a mediator do in a negotiation? It is not easy to spell this out. Peter Seitz has written: "As well ask a doctor how he cures the sick as ask a successful mediator how he works. Frequently, although flushed with success and satisfied with a job well done, he doesn't have the vaguest idea as to how it all came about. If he is sincere and brutally truthful with himself, he may admit that he does not know whether he was the moving cause of agreement or whether agreement was reached despite his efforts." (117) In an informational pamphlet, the Service says: "The mediator's job is *not to decide issues,* but to help the parties reconcile any differences which may exist between them." (118) His work is done in private and joint mediation sessions.

In the private meetings, the mediator talks freely with the negotiators from one or the other side and tries to find out what their positions are. Having determined this, he is in a position to seek a common ground of mutual accommodation. In most instances private mediation sessions, with the mediator traveling back and forth between the parties, are by far the most fruitful arrangement.

When the joint session is in progress, the mediator generally lets the parties present their positions. He tries to get all the issues out on the table. Having done this, he can decide on his course of action. Merely keeping tempers down and minds open is in itself an ambitious undertaking.

It is easy to understand why the joint session is often less productive than the private meetings. Each side is likely to present its position with great passion. Charges and countercharges are made, tempers begin to fray, and issues supposedly settled begin to come up again. It is no wonder that it is often practically impossible to reach an agreement in a face-to-face meeting between the parties. The mediation session normally consists of a series of private and joint meetings in which the mediator tries to help the parties narrow their differences and finally reach agreement.

To be effective, a mediator must have the confidence of the negotiators for both union and management, although simply having their confidence is not enough. He cannot be effective unless they confide in him and give him something to work with. A critical time in any negotiation occurs when both parties take positions from which they are determined not to move and from which someone must move if there is to be eventual agreement. In this situation, both parties generally recognize the value of a mediator, who serves an important function by providing a way for both sides to save face and continue with bargaining. When negotiations reach an impasse, the mediator is the ideal vehicle for moving the talks off dead center. Although not empowered with any legal force, he uses the quasi-power of moral persuasion. With the mediator on the scene, the union representatives can go back and tell their membership that a government representative is now in the picture and their previous positions may have to be altered.

The management representatives can go to their superiors and say the same. Either or both sides can thus save face by using the mediator as a scapegoat.

Mediators vary in their methods of work, since mediation is an extension of the personality of the mediator. This idea was touched on in an article by Arthur S. Meyer:

> Mediation, being an art rather than a science, is essentially personal. The only mediation that a mediator really understands is his own. In the early days of the New York State Mediation Board we attempted mediation by committees and, in one instance, mediation by the entire Board. The plan we found to work badly. Speaking for myself, I soon discovered that other mediators would speak at the very moment I would have remained silent, pursue a line of inquiry that I would have dropped, frown when I would have laughed, and kept the parties together when I would have separated them. Of course, I do not mean that I was right and the other wrong. I only mean that we were different and that in the practice of a subtle art, you can no more collaborate with others than you can improvise music together. (119)

The mediator's actions are dictated by the particular situation; there are no hard and fast rules. He must be guided by intuition. Perhaps Meyer has best described it: "The sea that he sails in is only roughly charted and its changing contours are not clearly discernible. Worse still, he has no science of navigation, no fund inherited from the experience of others. He is a solitary artist recognizing, at most, a few guiding stars and depending mainly on his personal power of divination."

The effective mediator is impartial, but not necessarily neutral. He is not merely a badminton bird to be knocked back and forth between the parties. When he thinks a proposal is completely out of line, he tells the parties so. When the situation dictates, he offers positive leadership.

MEDIATION BY ARBITRATORS

In an astute paper presented at a meeting of the National Academy of Arbitrators, J. Noble Braden, then executive vice president of the American Arbitration Association (AAA), listed the major complaints received about the mediation and the arbitration process: (1) lengthy opinions; (2) excessive time taken in studying the record and preparing the decisions; (3) excessive hearing days, that is, a belief by the party that the arbitrator had protracted the hearing; (4) delays in rendering the award; and (5) attempted mediation by the arbitrator. (120)

With regard to attempted mediation, arbitrators have said that they felt they could make enduring contributions to the relationship between management and labor and that the role of an arbitrator offered too few satisfactions unless there was a chance for service beyond the mere calling of balls and strikes. It may be granted that under appropriate circumstances an arbitrator may find occasional opportunities to mediate disputes. At such times he may indulge his yearning to help the parties solve some of their nonarbitrable problems—but only if he is so appointed and authorized by both parties.

To the extent that arbitrators have been guilty of the temptation to enlarge improperly the scope of their jurisdiction, they must assume their share of the blame for criticism from the parties. The arbitration mechanism is solely a creature of the parties and can be tailored to their purposes. If a party considers a particular arbitrator's views too elastic or flexible, the remedy is not to reject arbitration, but to reject the arbitrator.

Arbitrators were not made a part of the grievance procedure because companies and unions loved them. Arbitration of grievances is a lesser evil than strike or lockout. When the parties want an arbitrator, they find an arbitrator. When the parties want a mediator, they seek and find a mediator.

It is true that in some agreements the terminal point of the grievance procedure is mediation by an outside impartial agency, usually FMCS or a state mediation service. Some insist on the use of conciliation services as a regular part of their full adjustment procedure, while others make it optional. In other agreements, mediation is an intermediate step prior to arbitration, and some of these provide that mediation may be omitted and arbitration invoked immediately by mutual consent. A few agreements provide for mediation only on nonarbitrable issues.

A clause providing for mediation as a condition for arbitration reads as follows: "In the event that the employer and the union fail to adjust a grievance arising under this grievance procedure the parties, before resorting to the arbitration procedure provided in this agreement, mutually agree to request the services of governmental conciliation, mediation, or other appropriate Government agency in an effort to settle such grievance. In the event that the grievance is not settled through the aid of such conciliation or mediation, any further proceedings shall be dealt with in accordance with the provisions of Article ____ Arbitration." It should be noted that even here, where they have provided for a mediation effort preceding arbitration, the parties have nevertheless separated the process of seeking mutual accommodation from that of arranging for a binding settlement.

There are infrequent occasions when the parties will actually provide for an arbitrator to "wear two hats," as in the following example:

> Whenever either party concludes that further conferences in the procedure set forth in Step 4 cannot settle the grievance, such party may, not later than ten (10) days from the date of the last Step 4 meeting on the grievance, refer the grievance to the New York State Board of Mediation, hereinafter referred to as the board.
>
> This reference shall be in writing and shall be served upon the board and the other party. Upon receipt of such reference the board shall appoint an arbitrator to act upon the grievance. The arbitrator shall first try to mediate the grievance, but if this cannot be done, he shall arbitrate the grievance.

The vast majority of contracts do not make provision for any form of mediation within the grievance procedure. Those that do, however, separate the mediation effort and the principal performing it from the arbitration function and the neutral performing it. Seldom is one individual charged, as in the above clause, with the two functions. Even here, where they have chosen the same informed third party to serve in both capacities in the resolving of their differences, the parties have segregated his mediation duty from his arbitration duty.

Arbitrator Marion Beatty has defined the role of the arbitrator as follows: "In grievance arbitrations, arbitrators are employed to interpret contracts, not to write them, add to them or modify them. If they are to be modified, that has to be done at the bargaining table." (121) Most employers, and unions as well, would subscribe to this philosophy as it applies to attempts at mediation by arbiters.

The mediator and the arbitrator have distinct functions and objectives. The mediator is indifferent when it comes to dispute resolution. The contract is disregarded. His efforts are the products of mixed considerations, economic and political, measurable and immeasurable, rational and irrational. Mediation, like bargaining, often defies logic. One thing is traded for another, with accommodation and compromise the bywords.

By taking the arbitration route, the parties choose the uncertainty of an arbitral settlement in preference to the costs and risks of enlarging an agreement or tampering with its contents. Grievance arbitration departs from the flexibility of bargaining because of the signal importance of the contract. This document creates the grievance system, defines the authority of the arbitrator, and typically fixes substantive limits to the range of his decision making.

Three basic types of grievance matters reach the arbitrator: (1) those involving conduct explicitly permitted or denied by the contract; (2) those invoked by vague or ambiguous language or by conflicting clauses in the contract; and (3) those with which the contract fails to deal. With the first type, the clarity of the contract reduces the arbitrator's function to that of fact finder. The facts fall either within or outside the limits of the contract. He has no choice but to comply with its language. With the second (probably the source of most grievance arbitrations), he can exercise considerable judgment. With the last, he must depend upon the source of his authority. If the parties limit his jurisdiction to the interpretation or application of the agreement, he obviously cannot rule on something beyond its scope. If they impose no such restriction, he is free to consider the equities.

From the point of view of the employer, mediation by an arbitrator undermines the prevailing labor agreement and has an adverse effect on collective bargaining. When a dispute arises during the term of a collectively bargained agreement, the only question is whether the employer's action or inaction violated the provisions of the agreement. If there can be some mutually satisfactory settlement of the opened issue, between the parties and within the grievance machinery, before the arbitrator enters the picture, all that is well and good. But having failed in that regard, and having summoned their outside neutral, they are then seeking and are entitled to a final decision that puts to an end their haggling and compromising.

A proper conception of the arbitrator's function is basic. He is not a public tribunal imposed upon the parties by superior authority which the parties are obliged to accept. He has no general charter to administer justice for a community that transcends the parties. He is, rather, part of a system of self-government, created by and confined to the parties. He serves their pleasure only, to administer the rule of law established by their collective agreement. They are entitled to demand that, at least on balance, his performance be satisfactory to them, and they can readily dispense with him if it is not.

7

Arbitrability

THE question of the arbitrability of given issues is considered in about one of every ten arbitration clauses in manufacturing agreements and one of every eight in nonmanufacturing contracts. Both of these figures represent substantial increases over the corresponding percentages of only a few years ago. Most such provisions state that the question of arbitrability is one for the arbitral umpire himself to decide. A very few require a court proceeding to determine the question of arbitrability. (122)

A contract with the Ladies' Garment Workers, for example, includes a clause that gives exclusive jurisdiction to the arbitrator: "If any question or issue should arise concerning the validity of any clause of this agreement or the arbitrability (substantive or procedural) of any complaint, dispute or grievance thereunder, the Impartial Chairman shall have exclusive jurisdiction to determine such question, issue or matter and his decision shall be final and binding." (123) This provision would appear to foreclose either party from initially or even subsequently referring the question of arbitrability to the court.

As mentioned previously, a few collective bargaining agreements provide that such questions be referred to court. In the following example, that is the requirement unless the parties agree to do otherwise: "Any dispute as to the arbitrability of a given matter shall be resolved by a court of competent jurisdiction *and not by an arbitrator,* unless the parties specifically agree otherwise in writing." (emphasis added) (124)

In still another arrangement, either party appears to be able to seek a judicial determination, but only after an arbitrator has submitted his decision:

> If the Company believes the stated dispute is not arbitrable, it shall advise the union within five working days after receipt of the request for arbitration, stating its reasons therefor. If the Union decides to proceed with the arbitration, it will advise the Company in writing within five working days after receipt of the Company's notice that the Company believes the dispute is not arbitrable. The arbitration will proceed in the following manner:
>
> *a*) The arbitrator will be required to rule first on the arbitrability. If he finds in the affirmative, he shall then rule on the merits of the grievance at issue.
>
> *b*) If either party challenges the arbitrator's finding regarding the arbitrability, it may within thirty calendar days after receipt of the award, file suit in a court of competent jurisdiction to seek a judicial determination of the arbitrability of the subject matter. The Court in its determination shall be entitled to treat the matter as though originally submitted to it and neither the record of the arbitration nor the finding of the arbitrator shall be given any consideration by the court. (125)

This clause appears to give to the party contesting the arbitrability of the grievance "two bites at the apple," one before an arbitrator and, if that is lost, again before a court. Few agreements make such elaborate arrangements beforehand; only about one in ten mention the method to be employed to obtain final disposition of any question of arbitrability. This does not mean that parties without contract coverage are left without avenues of relief; it merely means that they either have not contemplated the problem or have not formalized an agreed-upon approach for disposing of such an issue.

First, complaints about the contract should not be steered toward the courts if there is no question of substantive or procedural problems not within the arbitrator's jurisdiction and authority. In most instances, the court will merely refer the matter back to the parties and the arbitration process, particularly if the contract and its grievance and arbitration provisions cover the dispute.

The law of the Steelworkers Trilogy is predicated in part upon the proposition that labor arbitrators are better equipped than judges to deal with questions of contract interpretion. (126) Chief Justice Douglas's opinion in *Warrior and Gulf* tells us that arbitrators perform functions that are "not normal to the courts," that the considerations that help arbitrators fashion judgments may be "foreign to the competence of the courts," and that arbitrators have a knowledge of "industrial common law" and the effects of a particular measure on productivity, shop morale, and intraplant tensions, which even the ablest judge cannot be expected to bring to bear upon the determination of contract questions.

These were not the only remarks of the Court on the subject of arbitral jurisdiction and authority. The Supreme Court has also stated that grievances are not to be compelled to arbitration when they are "so plainly unreasonable that the subject matter of the dispute must be regarded as nonarbitrable because it can be seen in advance that no award to the union would receive judicial sanction." (127)

A collective bargaining agreement typically has a dual purpose: (1) it fixes the substantive terms of employment to prevail in the enterprise, and (2) it establishes the procedural means for resolving disputes arising from the interpretation or application of those terms.

Despite the Steelworkers Trilogy opinions, in the case of *Enterprise Wheel and Car* the Court offered a word of caution: "An arbitrator is confined to interpretation and application of the collective bargaining agreement; *he does not sit to dispense his own brand of industrial justice.* He may of course look for guidance from many sources yet *his award is legitimate only so long as it draws its essence* from the collective bargaining agreement. When the arbitrator's words manifest an infidelity to this obligation, courts have no choice but to refuse enforcement of the award." (emphasis added) (128)

In summary, it can be said that unless the parties expressly exclude a matter from arbitration, the court will conclude that they intended to make it subject to arbitration. Therefore, it appears to be well established that the federal courts are limited to determining whether a contract between the parties which contains an arbitration clause is in force, whether there has been a violation of that labor agreement, and whether the violation is within the scope of the contract. Further, in considering whether to issue an order compelling arbitration, the courts have been instructed by the United States Supreme Court not to inquire into the merits of the grievance, but to determine whether the claim itself is covered by the contract.

In addition to these general principles, in subsequent cases, the courts have established certain specific criteria for determining whether arbitration should be ordered. Taken together, these cases comprise a new body of law covering arbitrability. Briefly stated, these cases establish:

> 1. If a contract has an arbitration clause and if the contract covers the subject matter in dispute, the court should order arbitration without considering the merits of the claim.
>
> 2. An award limited to the "interpretation and application of the collective bargaining agreement" will be enforced without any review by the court of the reasoning leading to that award.
>
> 3. Issues of damages for violation of a no-strike clause will be treated by the courts in the same manner as any other issue. That is, the court will decide whether the parties agreed in their contract to have such issues decided by the arbitration process. If they have, the issue will be arbitrated. If not, the court will decide it.
>
> 4. The arbitrator, not the courts, decides issues concerning whether there has been compliance with the contract's procedural requirements, which is a condition for hearing the case on its merits.
>
> 5. State courts have concurrent jurisdiction with the federal courts in suits for breaches of agreement. But the state courts must apply federal law in any situation in which the state and federal laws are in conflict.
>
> 6. An award which is beyond the scope of the collective-bargaining agreement may be set aside by the courts. However, the courts may not review the reasoning pursued by the arbitrator in making the award. (129)

A promise to submit grievances arising from the interpretation or application of the agreement to arbitration presents two separate questions of arbitrability. First, resistance to arbitration may be based on the claim that particular subject matters have been excluded from the promise to arbitrate—for example, the grant of a merit increase, the discharge of an employee for cause, the contracting out of work, the methods of performing an operation. The assertion is that a claimed violation of a claimed substantive rule is not within the purview of the arbitration commitment. It presents a question of substantive arbitrability. Is the subject within or without the promise to arbitrate?

Second, resistance to arbitration may be based on the claim that the steps preliminary to arbitration have not been followed—that the grievance was not submitted within a time limit, the time prescribed for taking the grievance from step to step was exceeded, or arbitration was not requested in the proper manner or within a certain time period. This would present a question of procedural arbitrability. Was there compliance with the conditions precedent to arbitration? (130)

Since the disputes fall under the umbrellas of two general categories, substantive and procedural, the following cases are cited to illustrate how arbitrators have dealt with the questions in the arbitrational forum.

MEETING PRECEDENT CONDITIONS

There are any number of contractual provisions that could impose conditions on one or the other party as the case develops and proceeds toward eventual arbitration. For example, a contract states that a grievance must be filed within ten days of the occurrence of the event on which it is based, and one is filed six months after the event—and also after the union had knowledge of it. The company takes the position that the grievance is untimely. In view of the contention of procedural defectiveness, is it arbitrable?

The contract states that the employee must be signatory to his grievance. A grievance is signed by a union committeeman on the employee's behalf. Is it arbitrable, or has it failed to meet a mandatory condition, which renders it null?

In a four-step grievance procedure, the union demands arbitration immediately after filing its complaint, skipping all of the contractual steps. Will it ultimately prove to be nonarbitrable because of the procedural irregularity?

In the absence of a specified time limit for invoking arbitration, is a reasonable time to be inferred? What constitutes a reasonable time?

It is plain that questions of procedure deal with the minutiae of the arbitration process. They are the details of a scheme that, in its overall aspect, is taken for granted as the method of dispute settlement. Questions of contract interpretation are subsumed under the uncontested promise to arbitrate unsettled grievances. For example, the question of whether a reasonable time limit to invoke arbitration is to be assumed in the absence of a specifically prescribed time is answered, in major part, by a judgment about the function of grievance handling. A valid judgment may be that a grievance should be handled promptly or be considered dropped; avoidable delay in its prosecution should be discouraged; dilatory handling allows an unhealthy accumulation of stale grievances. If so, it follows that arbitration should be invoked within a reasonable time or not at all. And this is a value subsumed under the arbitral scheme. Similarly, questions of fact are highly particularized. What constitutes a reasonable time, for example, is almost entirely related to the special circumstances of the individual situation. (131)

The ways in which some of these procedural questions have been answered by arbitrators is worth reviewing. Although a grievance may be procedurally defective, the defect may be excused and therefore have no effect on the validity of the claim if it is not challenged in time. At McLouth Steel Corporation, an arbitrator refused to dismiss a grievance for not having been filed according to the contract when the protest against improper filing was not made until the arbitration hearing. It was held that procedural issues of this nature were ordinarily considered to have been waived if not raised in the previous grievance steps. (132) A review of a large number of published decisions shows that a preponderance of arbitrators have concurred with this concept. (133)

With clear contract language delineating the proper grievance process, most arbitrators will rule that the parties themselves have established the procedural requirements to be observed. However, failure to protest an infraction in time can result in the company's forfeiture. On this point, arbitrator Langston T. Hawley ruled as follows:

> The company is also contending that the grievance should be dismissed because it is not signed, in accordance with Article XXIX, Section 1 of the Agreement by the aggrieved employee. The arbitrator believes that the grievance should be handled on its merits and not dismissed on technical grounds. This grievance was processed

through all steps of the contract prior to its submission to arbitration. The company had five months prior to the hearing to raise objection on the grounds now being urged and yet its first objection was made known to the union at the time of the hearing. In the light of these facts, the arbitrator believes that the signature on the grievance of an authorized representative of the aggrieved employee is sufficient. (134)

In addition to this type of procedural difficulty, where the employer had failed to contest the union's technical error, there are a variety of other types, a few of which merit examination. To demonstrate the contrasting rulings in two such cases, reference is made first to a decision by arbitrator Clare B. McDermott in a case between the U.S. Steel Corporation and the United Steelworkers:

> The grievance in Case USS–5145–H was filed by thirteen Grievance Committeemen, attempting to allege a violation of an obligation of ". . . the company to the Union as such," under Section 6–E, on behalf of all other unnamed employees who did not receive Labor Day holiday pay and who neither filed individual grievances nor signed one of the seven grievances in USS–5146–H.
>
> From the beginning, Management has insisted that this is an improper subject matter for a union grievance under Section 6–E. When the defect was pointed out in Step 3, the Union said it could name individual employees referred to and their particular circumstances, and the employees so identified. *No such identification was given.* Holiday pay provisions of the Agreement can be applied only in light of specific fact situations, which are of nearly infinite variety, some of which would qualify an employee for holiday pay and others of which would not. Thus, the grievance in USS–5145–H, *without stating the particular situations of any named, aggrieved employees, really does not present any holiday pay question which this Board can decide,* and does not ". . . allege a violation of; the obligations of the company to the union as such." Accordingly, it will be dismissed." [emphasis added] (135)

In contrast with this award, in another case, in which the facts were somewhat different, arbitrator Saúl Wallen found a grievance did meet the necessary procedural requirements with regard to being filed in sufficient detail. He stated:

> Article XXI, Section 7 (c) requires that a written grievance "be in such detail as to identify the nature of the complaint, the name of the aggrieved employee or employees, the date and the place of the

complaint." The company objects to the grievance on the grounds that it did not specifically list the names of the grievants but instead had a seniority roster of Operators appended to it. We find that the grievance filed is sufficiently definite for the company to identify the persons who actually were discharged and constituted sufficient notice of the union's challenge of that action. The inclusion of the names of those *not* discharged *does not* detract from the validity of the protest for those who were. Thus, the grievance meets the requirements of Section 7 (c). (136)

A careful examination of the two awards readily reveals the rationale employed by the two competent arbiters. Although the factual differences were not substantial, they were clearly sufficient to produce different findings.

In the next two cases, the question was whether a regulating agreement existed.

A grievance arose after a contract had expired and before the parties had agreed to abide by the old contract pending enactment of a new one. It was ruled arbitrable. The influencing factor was that a supervisor answered the grievance in accordance with contractual procedures after the parties had agreed to be bound by the old contract. This indicated to the arbitrator that the company was bound to arbitrate and that it should have felt itself obligated to follow each procedural step after the supervisor's "answer." (137)

In another situation, a discharge grievance was arbitrable even though the discharge occurred before the employer and the union had executed their contract. The circumstances were as follows: (1) the employer and the union had operated in accordance with the contracts in effect between other contractors and unions at the job site prior to signing their own identical agreement; (2) the union had attempted to settle the discharge dispute through contractual grievance procedures, and the employer had dealt with the union on that basis, thereby implicitly acknowledging that contract procedures were applicable; and, finally, (3) the employer did not raise the question of arbitrability prior to the arbitration hearing. (138) Even if this last factor had not been in the picture, it is doubtful that the outcome would have been much different, if at all.

Given the types of questions involved in procedural arbitrability, are they more properly resolved by judges or by arbitrators?

In *Livingston* v. *John Wiley and Sons,* the second court of appeals had this to say:

> Indeed, it may well be that the arbitrator can make his most impor-
> tant contribution to industrial peace by a fair, impartial and well-
> informed decision of these very procedural matters. To hold mat-
> ters of procedure to be beyond the competence of the arbitrator
> to decide, would, we think, rob the parties of the advantages they
> have bargained for, that is to say, the determination of the issues
> between them by an arbitrator and not by a court. A contrary deci-
> sion would emasculate the arbitration provisions of the contract. It
> is of the essence of arbitration that it be speedy and that the source
> of friction between the parties be promptly eliminated. . . . The
> numerous cases involving the great variety of procedural niceties
> . . . make it abundantly clear that, were we to decide that proce-
> dural questions under an arbitration clause of a collective bargain-
> ing agreement are for the court, we would open the door wide to
> all sorts of technical obstructionism. (139)

In other words, in separating the question of substantive arbitrability from that of procedural arbitrability, the promise to arbitrate
the merits of disputes evidences a fundamental commitment to the
arbitral process. One may therefore assume that the procedural
questions are secondary and have been entrusted to the arbitrator
as part of the whole scheme.

ISSUE INSIDE OR OUTSIDE ARBITRATION SCOPE

Perhaps the most frequently claimed basis for nonarbitrability
is that the issue is not covered by the contract and, therefore, the
arbitrator has no jurisdiction to hear the matter. The matters covered above dealt with issues involving questions of nonarbitrability
for procedural reasons. Those to be covered now deal with questions of nonarbitrability due to substantive preclusion.

In *Warrior and Gulf,* the company argued that a question of subcontracting was nonarbitrable on the basis that it was purely a
management function and not limited by the labor agreement. The
union argued that the company violated the contract by its action
of contracting out. The arbitration provision at Warrior and Gulf
read as follows:

> Issues which conflict with any federal statute in its application as
> established by Court procedure or matters which are strictly a func-

tion of management shall not be subject to arbitration under this section.

Should differences arise between the Company and the Union or its members employed by the Company as to the meaning and application of the provisions of this Agreement, or should any local trouble of any kind arise, there shall be no suspension of work on account of such differences but an earnest effort shall be made to settle such differences immediately in the following manner:

Fifth, if agreement has not been reached the matter shall be referred to an impartial umpire for decision. The parties shall meet to decide on an umpire acceptable to both. If no agreement on selection of an umpire is reached, the parties shall jointly petition the United States Conciliation Service for suggestion of a list of umpires from which selection will be made. The decision of the umpire shall be final.

The limitation embodied in this clause is primarily exposed in the particular phrase "or matters which are strictly a function of managment shall not be subject to arbitration under this section."

The Supreme Court said that such a limitation excluded only some issues from arbitration. Regrettably, for those seeking explicit or definitive distinctions, the exact boundaries of the exclusion are unclear. The Court stated: "Apart from matters that the parties specifically exclude, all of the questions on which the parties disagree must therefore come within the scope of the grievance and arbitration provisions of the collective agreement." What does this mean in effect and practice? Basically, the conclusion was that an arbitrator may determine what constitutes a management function. Whether a given activity is a "management function" is a question to be decided by the arbitration process because it involves a determination of the "meaning and application" of the contract.

The Court's ruling in no way vitiated the force of the management-rights clause. Rather, it assigned the issue to the proper forum to determine whether it was binding.

The scope of an arbitration clause may determine whether a matter is excluded from arbitration. The scope of the management—rights article and operating clauses may also influence whether the issue raises a substantive question. Essentially, the argument in *Warrior and Gulf* was that subcontracting was a matter outside the contract and, therefore, not within the arbitrator's jurisdiction. The function of the court is a limited one: it may determine only whether a party seeking arbitration is making a claim that on its face is governed by the contract. The arbitrators decide the merits of the question.

Decisions on substantive arbitrability may either uphold the claim or reject it as nonarbitrable on its merits. A sampling of both types is useful in order to discern the rationale behind them.

An employer demanded that the union be required to furnish to employees who were not union members the funeral benefits and free periodicals furnished to members. The company's theory was that the contract in general as well as the contract's union-security provisions implicitly or otherwise obligated the union to do so in consideration of the fact that such employees had to pay the union a sum equal to periodic dues paid by members. The arbitrator ruled that the claim was not arbitrable on the basis that the contract did not in express terms or by "any interpretation to which the language is susceptible" permit the arbitrator to confer on nonmembers the benefits that under the union's constitution were available to members only. (140)

Another employer's refusal to allow an employee to return to work after a two-year absence caused by a nonoccupational illness was not an arbitrable issue. Under the agreement, an employee who was not able to work due to nonoccupational illness was to remain on the payroll for a period of 90 days and "his status thereafter shall become a subject of negotiations between the company and the union." The contract merely required the employer to *negotiate* with the union concerning the return to work of the employee. Once that was done, as it had been here, the employer had no further obligation. The arbiter held that the contract did not require that such negotiations result in agreement or provide that failure to reach agreement was a matter for arbitration. (141)

Occasionally, the conduct or alleged misconduct of a management representative will provoke a grievance demanding that he be disciplined or ousted. And sometimes a supervisor's attitude and demeanor may leave much to be desired by both the employees and management. Of course, management should take the necessary and adequate steps within its own organization to censure and correct any instance of supervisory misconduct. However, in the overwhelming majority of such cases put before an arbitrator and the arbitrability of which was contested by management, the arbitrator has most often ruled against the union *unless* the parties had agreed by contract or otherwise to give him jurisdiction to decide the grievance on its merits.

Typical of commonsense arbitral rulings in this area was that in a case involving the King Powder Company, where a grievance demanded the discharge of a foreman for using abusive language and improperly docking wages. Arbitrator Dudley Whiting, an experienced and capable member of the National Academy of Arbitrators, commented as follows: "It is a fundamental principle of American industry that the selection and retention of foremen or other supervisory personnel is the sole prerogative of management, particularly where they are excluded from the benefits of the collective bargaining agreement covering other employees. There is no doubt that the union may not, as a matter of right, demand the dismissal or demotion of a foreman and that such a demand is not a proper subject matter for a grievance." (142)

To provide some balance to this analysis, and more importantly because arbitrability issues are often upheld, the following examples are offered in review.

Whether the employer had the right to retire an employee for reasons of age was considered an arbitrable issue under a contract defining "grievance" as "any dispute involving the effect, interpretation, application, claim of breach or violation" of the contract and allowing arbitration of any and all grievances so defined. The mere fact that the agreement contained no provision specifically dealing with the retirement question did not in itself preclude the matter from arbitration. (143)

A dispute over the employer's failure to grant maternity leaves to three employees was deemed arbitrable, notwithstanding the fact that pregnancy was not listed in the contract as one of the causes justifying a leave of absence. The deciding factor was that the subject of leaves as such was dealt with in the contract, and was, therefore, in the view of the arbitrator, a matter over which management did not have unlimited discretion. (144)

In a final example, the issue was whether an employee who had incurred injury in the course of his employment was entitled to the difference between his regular wages and workmen's compensation benefits. Despite the employer's claim that there was no provision in the agreement requiring such pay, the issue was held to be arbitrable because the contract allowed for arbitration of all differences, disputes, or grievances pertaining to the terms of the contract. However, the arbitrator made it clear that in passing on the question of arbitrability, he was not prejudging the issue itself. (145)

MERITS VERSUS THRESHOLD ISSUE

When the validity of a grievance is in question for procedural or substantive reasons there are two potential issues to be presented to the arbitrator. The first question is a *threshold matter:* Is the grievance procedurally or substantively faulty to a degree that renders it nonarbitrable? If it is deemed arbitrable, the next issue is whether the claim has sufficient merit to be sustained. Several results are feasible. If the employer is raising the procedural issue and seeking to have the grievance denied, both on the arbitrability question as well as on its merits, the company will have "two bites at the apple"—two opportunities to have an award in its favor. In such case, the union has to survive two tests in order to achieve its objective. Of course, the employer may lose on both counts. However, the point should be made that a grievance may raise technical questions about arbitrability and at the same time have intrinsic merits, with both facts recognized by the employer. For example, an employee may be discharged improperly and without sufficient cause—or without any cause at all for that matter; because of contractually improper processing and grievance handling, he may never have his case heard or decided on its merits by reason of it being deemed nonarbitrable. This is an example of one of the inequities of a system for which few mutually acceptable solutions have been found.

In order to have sufficient authority as provided for under the parties' contract, the arbitrator must be appointed in accordance with the terms of the contract. If his appointment does not square with those requirements, his authority may be invalid and his award unenforceable.

It will be remembered that under certain contracts an appointing agency is empowered to make an arbitral selection for the parties. If, in such a case, that agency does not accord with the contractual regulations, the appointment could be, and most likely would be, invalid. Also, if by the contractual arrangement it is merely to proffer names, the agency could not make an appointment in the face of one party's refusal to participate in the selection process. If the agency makes an appointment without the participation of one party, that party must then decide whether it will participate in a hearing or allow it to proceed ex parte (in his absence). If its position is that the appointment is procedurally invalid and therefore any award would not be enforceable, the courts would probably set aside an award upon such a showing. However, in view of the Steelworkers Trilogy and subsequent cases, it would appear that, if the appointment is procedurally correct and the arbitrator is satisfied after an ex parte hearing that the issue is arbitrable, the courts will be likely to refuse to review a claim that the subject matter was excluded from arbitration by the contract.

With regard to separating the threshold issue of arbitrability from the question of the merits of the grievance, some parties have provided contractual coverage. In one major labor agreement, the arbitrability of the dispute is to be decided before it is considered on its merits: "If either party shall claim before the Arbitrator that a particular grievance fails to meet the tests of arbitrability . . . the arbitrator shall proceed to decide such issue before proceeding to hear the case upon the merits. . . . In any case where the arbitrator determines that such grievance fails to meet said tests of arbitrability he shall refer the case back to the parties without a decision or recommendation on its merits." (146) This language appears to be clear in restraining the arbitrator from rendering a decision or opinion on the merits of a case that he has found nonarbitrable. However, it may leave certain other questions unanswered.

One may infer from the contract that both issues—arbitrability and merits, as well as the arguments for and against them—are to be presented to the arbitrator at one and the same hearing.

In other words, can the threshold issue of arbitrability be presented in an initial hearing, separate and apart from a hearing on merits? Can an award be rendered on that issue alone before the arbitrator hears anything whatsoever about the parties' respective positions with regard to merits? Granted, such procedure would require two separate hearings. However, such an approach is often in the best interests of the party contesting the arbitrability of the grievance. It must also be acknowledged that more often than not the arbitrator will prefer to consider both issues at one time, thus saving himself time and travel. As a consequence, he may render a decision on the threshold matter without going into the merits. The arbitrator, however, is a servant to the parties; if their mandate is that the issues be heard separately, he must abide by that arrangement.

Dividing the case into two distinct hearings is sometimes viewed as desirable for psychological reasons. The arbitrator would not be influenced by the merits of the case while considering the purely technical arguments about arbitrability. Arbitrators are only human after all. After having heard both cases in full, the arbitrator would have to have a well-disciplined mind and a stable emotional constitution to keep the two issues segregated and to resist the temptation of finding a case with merits arbitrable if his ruling to the contrary would render it null. The closer the decision on arbitrability, surely the more difficult it is for the arbitrator to rule a case nonarbitrable when it appears to have substantive merits.

These are valid considerations when the parties weigh a decision to combine or separate the issues.

The parties may mutually agree to arrange for two hearings. If so, the arbitrator is originally presented with only the parties' respective positions, arguments, and evidence, on the procedural or substantive arbitrability question. Nothing relating to merits is revealed—or only so much as is essential and necessary to deal with the question of threshold. The hearing is closed, and only if the arbitral finding is in favor of arbitrability is another hearing necessary. Also, if it is deemed arbitrable, the parties may then choose to present the dispute on its merits to a different arbitrator.

There is one other adversary approach to handling this question of presentation of threshold issue versus presentation of merits. It involves some willingness to engage in brinkmanship.

Again, it has to do with an ex parte hearing. If management is adamant in its desire to deal with the two issues in two separate hearings, it should advise the union of its stand during grievance processing and prearbitration discussions. This should be made clear to the agency making the arbitral selection or submitting panels of names. It should be made clear to the selected arbitrator, before and during the hearing on the threshold question. He should be advised that he has not been selected to consider the merits of the dispute or empowered to do so. He should be advised at the outset of the hearing of the party's intention to withdraw at the close of the hearing on that single, initial issue and of the party's refusal to be bound by any decision that may be subsequently rendered in an ex parte proceeding. At the appropriate time, the party should leave—and pray a little of course. There are risks involved, but attaining most things worthwhile involves taking some risks.

In the majority of instances, the arbitrator will try to persuade the parties to do it all in one sitting. That is understandable. Also, in the majority of cases, it is unlikely that he will proceed with a hearing at which one party is absent, especially if there is any doubt about his having been given jurisdiction over the second issue. However, if he has been given jurisdiction over that issue, the party is foolhardy to attempt this approach, and its chances for a favorable outcome are extremely doubtful. Under those circumstances, being absent at an ex parte hearing is not brinksmanship, but hara-kiri.

The procedural question is, of course, whether the arbiter should rule on arbitrability before either party presents its case with regard to merits, or whether he should reserve his conclusions on the threshold question until the full case, including merits, has been completely presented.

In summary, it is well to examine the comments of professionals from different schools of thought.

Arbitrator Harry Dworkin believes that the ruling on arbitrability should be made before the presentation of the case on the merits: "The Chairman is of the opinion that when a party raises the issue of arbitrability, it is better practice to pass upon this issue at the time it is presented, and before hearing the dispute on the merits, for the reason that whenever possible, parties should have the right to an interim decision or ruling on any question presented during the course of the hearing, and that this procedure is preferable to the reservation of the ruling until after the conclusion of the hearing." (147)

Arbitrator Douglas B. Maggs is a spokesman for the point of view that the ruling on arbitrability may be reserved until the full case has been heard. In a dispute involving Barbet Mills, Inc., he remarked:

> The arbitrator may properly reserve his ruling upon arbitrability until after he has heard evidence and argument upon its merits. A contrary rule would cause needless delay and expense, necessitating two hearings whenever the arbitrator needed time to consider the question of arbitrability. Furthermore, in many cases, it is only after

a hearing on the merits has informed the arbitrator of the nature of the dispute that he is in a position to determine whether it is of the kind covered by the agreement to arbitrate. . . . This procedure does not, of course, preclude the party who loses from obtaining any judicial review of the arbitrator's decision to which it is entitled by law; to reassure the company about this I explicitly rule that its participation in the hearing upon the merits would not constitute a waiver of its objections to arbitrability." (148)

Dworkin and Maggs have clearly expressed different points of view on this question. As advocate and as arbitrator, the author has held both points of view, depending upon the role he was playing at the time. As advocate, he favored Dworkin's view, almost always urging the arbitrator to rule in favor of a total separation of the issues. However, when looking at the question from the vantage point of the arbitrator, he was most often inclined to follow Maggs's concept. This would seem to demonstrate, at least in part, that one's position on this particular question is somewhat influenced by the chair he is occupying at the arbitral hearing table.

However, there is a commonsense middle ground between these two positions: the choice should be based on consideration of all the circumstances of the particular dispute. This procedure is followed by the Connecticut State Board of Mediation, which states:

> The Board will inform the party protesting arbitrability that it will be permitted to raise that issue at the hearing. The Board will then first hear arguments on arbitrability before it proceeds to the merits of the dispute. The Board makes clear that at the hearing both parties must be prepared to proceed on the merits after the Board has heard them on arbitrability.
>
> After the case on arbitrability has been presented, the Board will assess the circumstances then obtaining to determine if it will proceed directly to the merits.
>
> Under its policy, the Board reserves the right either to require the parties to go forward on the merits at the same hearing or to determine that the decision on arbitrability should be made first before proceeding on the merits." (149)

This is certainly a more flexible arrangement. It attempts to ensure that each decision about whether to separate the two aspects, threshold and merits, is based on the peculiar facts of the case. Nevertheless, it too fails to meet the special needs of the party definitely committed to the separation of issues or one determined to see them treated together.

In any case, the overwhelming majority of published conclusions shows that arbitrators customarily separate the two issues in their written opinions, putting the question of arbitrability and its answer before the discussion and conclusion on the merits of the case.

8

Interpreting the Agreement

THE arbitrator has many duties and responsibilities, among which none can be considered more important than interpreting the labor agreement. A party faced with the challenge of arbitrating a dispute is well advised to become familiar with the manner in which arbitrators approach and handle this entire area. Since the great majority of arbitration cases involve questions of "rights" under labor contracts, the agreement itself is the focal point of attention, calling into action the powers of the arbitrator to interpret and construe its intended meanings. The purpose of this chapter is to provide an overview of the generally established rules of contract interpretation and application, based on published decisions.

First, a well-established rule of law, frequently invoked by industrial arbitrators, is that the collective bargaining agreement, like any other written instrument, must be construed as a whole. Single words, sentences, or sections cannot be isolated from the context in which they appear and interpreted independently of the apparent purpose and understanding of the parties as evidenced by the entire instrument. (150)

For example, the commonly accepted meaning of the word "recall," which appears in many contracts is management's offer to an employee of the opportunity to return to work. One definition is: "Recall is part of the process of rehiring following layoff. The term refers to the employers' action in inviting those laid off to return to work." However, in some agreements, the term refers to offering an open job to the employee who formerly held it but who is currently working in another classification. In other agreements, it may mean something else. The number and variety of terms usually found in labor agreements are nearly as endless as their possible definitions.

In deciding on the proper interpretation, one should be mindful of the recognized canons of contract construction. The principles are supported by ample authority. One arbitrator has remarked: "It is a cardinal rule of contract interpretation that the Agreement must be so construed as to give effect to all of its provisions. An arbitrator is not justified in reading a portion of the contract provisions out of the Agreement where it is possible to give effect to each provision therein included. There is also a well settled rule of construction that the "specific" provision must be given effect in the interpretation of the contract." (151)

In their excellent book, *How Arbitration Works,* Elkouri and El-kouri stated: "If an arbitrator finds that alternative interpretations of a clause are possible, one of which would give meaning and effect to another provision of the contract, while the other would render the other provision meaningless or ineffective, he will be inclined to use the interpretation which would give effect to all provisions."

However, conclusions should not run counter to the principles of reason and equity. If examination of the entire agreement reveals that management's action violates other contractual provisions, the employer should readily admit its error. Further, the contract provisions that the union alleges were violated *may or may not be* relevant to the dispute. This does not mean that a contract violation has not occurred or that the grievance should be denied because of the union's erroneous citation. Although the clause cited may not have specific application, conceivably an examination of the agreement may reveal other contractual provisions that are pertinent. Also, the fact that a written grievance does not cite the contract clause violated will probably not bar arbitration if the contract makes no specific requirement to that effect. (152)

In a case involving the Glamorgan Pipe and Foundry Company, the union cited a section of the contract's seniority article other than the relevant one section permitting employees to exercise seniority in making lateral transfers to vacant jobs. Arbitrator Donald A. Crawford held that that did not constitute sufficient cause to dismiss the grievance protesting the employer's failure to permit such a transfer, inasmuch as the section cited stated that the employer "shall recognize company and departmental seniority" and the employer's failure to do so in this case was in violation of that section. (153)

It may also be well to state here that, when called upon to construe the meaning and intent of a labor agreement, the courts use accepted standards of general application. (154)

The rules of contract construction are equally as applicable to labor agreements as they are to commercial contracts. No less care should therefore be exercised in drafting them or the consequences may be both economically and operationally injurious. Arbitrators follow the same standards of construction. To say it more plainly, it should be recognized that all written instruments, constitutions, statutes, and contracts are interpreted by the same general principles, although the specific subject matter may call for strictness or liberality. (155)

Any doubts on the part of management with regard to the meaning of contractual terms should lead to further investigation and analysis. More often than is desirable, it may be learned that the same provision has been interpreted and administered differently from supervisor to supervisor, department head to department head, shift to shift.

If the contract language is clear and explicit, it may permit only one persuasion. Typically, however, contract clauses are drawn up by draftsmen of varying skills; as a result, they may be susceptible of more than one interpretation, any one of which might be persuasively argued. On the other hand, the contract may be entirely silent on the disputed matter, bringing to the fore management's position on residual rights.

One of the defenses sometimes put forth by management is a provision commonly called the "zipper clause," which hopefully precludes it from bargaining on "uncovered" issues during the term of the agreement. The term "hopefully" is used here because the force and effect accorded this clause by the NLRB as a waiver specific enough to remove the obligation to bargain may turn on the particular fact situation, the circumstances involved, and the particular wording of the contract. The following is fairly typical of a "zipper clause" provision, but, there are, of course, numerous variations:

> The parties acknowledge that during the negotiations which resulted in this Agreement each had unlimited right and opportunity to make demands and proposals with respect to any subject or matter not removed by law from the area of collective bargaining, and that the understandings and agreements arrived at by the Parties after exercise of that right and opportunity are set forth and solely embodied in this Agreement.

> Therefore the Corporation and the Union, for the life of this Agreement, each voluntarily and unqualifiedly waives the right, and each agree that the other shall not be obligated, to bargain collectively with respect to any subject matter referred to or covered in this Agreement, or with respect to any subject matter not specifically referred to or covered in this Agreement, even though such subjects or matters may not have been within the knowledge or contemplation of either or both of the Parties at the time they negotiated or signed this Agreement.

Assuming that such a clause is in the contract and that the grievance dispute involves some "uncovered" subject matter, some employers refer to this provision as one of their defenses, arguing that the union is attempting to obtain through grievance and arbitration that which they either did not attempt or did not obtain in the course of bargaining.

However, a silent contract does not *necessarily* dictate that such matters are automatically resolved in the employer's favor. Contract language may cover a matter in a general way but fail to cover all of its aspects—that is, gaps sometimes exist. Or the matter may not be covered in any fashion by any contract clause. In such an instance, custom and past practice may constitute a significant factor in the dispute. For this reason, and because of the significance of customs and practices, the following section is devoted to gap filling.

In the authoritative work of Elkouri and Elkouri, this appropriate analysis was made:

> Some gap-filling is a natural part of the interpretive process. Situations unforeseen when the agreement was written, but falling within

its general framework, often arise. Arbitrators considering these situations may decide, insofar as possible, what the parties would have agreed upon, within the general framework of the agreement, had the matter been specifically before them. (156)

At least as long as gap-filling is primarily a matter of interpretation or application of what does appear in the contract, it should not be deemed prohibited. (157)

Gap-filling, however, is improper (unless authorized) when it results in a basic addition to, subtraction from, or modification of the agreement. (158)

Such is the general rationale of reputable arbitrators in dealing with vagueness or with uncovered subjects. In the remaining sections of this chapter, the primary criteria observed by the majority of arbitrators in determining the meaning and intent of contract language will be explored.

Two last examples provide further insights. In a case involving the Kroger Company, the union complained that the employer violated the contract in assigning employees in one job classification to do work in another classification for approximately a day or less. The union testified that it had understood in negotiations that classification integrity would be observed. Despite the fact that another grievance settlement had apparently supported the principle of the union's case, the arbitrator ruled in favor of the company. He held that he might consider bargaining-table statements and grievance settlements *only as an aid* in resolving ambiguities in negotiated language, but the contract here was completely silent on any restriction on the company's right to assign job duties. (159)

At the Container Corporation of America, the contract stated that unworked holidays would be counted as days worked for purposes of computing weekly overtime. Employees who had a three-day Christmas holiday, pursuant to the contract, were ruled to be entitled to special overtime premiums for work performed on the following Saturday and Sunday. The parties were bound by the contract as written, despite the company's contention that the contract, as signed, omitted agreed-upon language limiting holidays that should be considered as days worked to those on which the employee otherwise would have been scheduled to work. This was the holding based on the following factors: (1) there was no evidence of clear and unmistakable intention of the parties to qualify the contract; (2) the alleged mistake was unilateral on the part of the employer who drafted the final agreement, and not a mutual mistake; and (3) there was no "true" contract, agreed to by the negotiators and approved by the union and management officials who were authorized to accept or reject the final agreement, which the arbitrator might substitute for the written contract. (160)

CLEAR AND UNAMBIGUOUS LANGUAGE

The best evidence of what the parties willed or intended is in the language of the labor agreement itself, which, if direct and unambiguous, will customarily be interpreted accordingly by arbitrators. (161) What is important is the impression the words make and leave. This can best be understood by realizing that although each contractual statement may be clear and certain as it stands alone, the consolidation of all the provisions into a whole can produce a doubtful result because of a lack of harmony in its various parts. (162)

It is not possible to write language sufficiently clear and comprehensive to cover all the numerous and various situations and questions that may arise during the life of an agreement. That is one of the reasons for the dispute-resolving machinery of grievance and arbitration processes. What may be clear to one person may be ambiguous to another. What is in the mind and eye of one reader may be perceived differently by another. While the contract that governs their relationship is presumably comprehensive, it is viewed necessarily as a flexible document by sophisticated labor negotiators. (163) On this point, one arbitrator quoted Justice Holmes: "A word is not a crystal, transparent and unchanged; it is the skin of a living thought and may vary greatly in color and content according to the circumstances and the time in which it is used." (164)

The arbitrator's primary objective is to determine what the parties meant to say and intended to do and then apply the language of the labor agreement in such a way as to carry out the joint intent of the parties. Where the language is susceptible to only one interpretation, his job is certainly made simpler. More often than not, the contractual language is not that definite and certain, and, of course, that is one of the reasons the parties are in dispute. Where the language is vague or ambiguous, interpretations are more difficult.

Ambiguities in contractual expressions may result from various factors. One such is poor draftsmanship. The parties may have erroneously believed that they were clearly expressing their mutual desires. When their agreement is applied to a real-life circumstance, however, they realize it can be interpreted in more than one way. Such a discovery may provide too much temptation to an opportunistically motivated party and lead to its applying an interpretation compatible with its present interests, but different from the one originally intended. On the other hand, ambiguity in language may be intentional. Sometimes when they cannot reach a conclusive meeting of minds on an issue, rather than remain at an impasse, and in order to save face by not submitting to each others' position, the parties will draft language that each knows is susceptible to the preferred interpretation of the other. The result is that the confrontation is only postponed until later, when it must be dealt with in grievance and arbitration proceedings. The arbitrator selected at that time is put in the position of sifting through the counterclaims and contentions. Often, in such cases, his interpretation is one that he believes will provide the greatest degree of justice and equity. Sometimes he puts the matter back into the laps of the parties for further bargaining. (165) On the other hand, if the arbitrator is given the authority by the parties to decide the issue, his evaluation will be conclusive. (166)

The primary factor in contract interpretation is determining the intent of the parties at the time of the negotiation of the clause(s) at issue, rather than reading an interpretation into the contested provision. (167)

An article in *American Jurisprudence* puts the governing rule with regard to the "intent of the parties" as follows:

> Whatever may be the inaccuracy of expression or the ineptness of words used in an instrument in a legal view, if the intention of the parties can be clearly discovered, the court will give effect to it and construe the words accordingly. It must not be supposed, however, that an attempt is made to ascertain the actual mental processes of the parties to a particular contract. The law presumes that the parties understood the import of their contract and that they had the intention which its terms manifest. It is not within the function of the judiciary to look outside of the instrument to get at the intention

of the parties and then carry out that intention regardless of whether the instrument contains language sufficient to express it; but their sole duty is to find out what was meant by the language of the instrument. This language must be sufficient, when looked at in the light of such facts as the court is entitled to consider, to sustain whatever effect is given to the instrument. (168)

Where the language is clear and unambiguous, the arbiter may disregard the equities of the matter—which could bring him to a different decision—and apply instead the logical interpretation of the disputed provision(s). (169) The interpretation of words clearly susceptible to only one conclusion may produce an undesirable consequence—even one rough on one or both parties—but such may be a legitimate arbitral conclusion. (170) The parties are presumed to be responsible for what they have agreed upon, and an arbitrator should not be blamed for faults that originated with the parties themselves

Some examples of how arbitrators have handled both clear and vague contract language will provide helpful insight into this problem.

A contract clause stated: "After an employee is scheduled for a bi-weekly period he will not be laid-off or required to work less than the normal 80 hours for such bi-weekly periods." The arbitrator held that the clause constituted an 80-hour, biweekly pay guarantee for each scheduled employee. He felt he had to give literal effect to the contract language since the parties had come to no meeting of the minds on the provision and past practice was inconclusive. However, since the union acknowledged that no absolute pay guarantee was intended, the appropriate grievance committeeman might agree to scheduling a shorter biweekly period. But, without such an agreement, it was ruled that the employer had to (1) pay an employee for 80 hours even though the schedule called for less than that much work, and (2) to lay off junior employees in order to provide 80-hour biweekly schedules for senior employees. (171)

At the Goodyear Atomic Corporation the labor agreement provided that if employees were not permitted a lunch period "they shall be paid at time and one-half for the time worked in excess of eight hours." An employee's nonpaid lunch period was interrupted to perform work assigned by his supervisor, and he was not provided a rescheduled noninterrupted lunch period later. In view of the explicit wording, arbitrator Walter Seinsheimer ruled that the employee was entitled to overtime pay for 30 minutes. (172)

The agreement at the Wheland Company provided that a paid lunch period would be granted to all employees "should the company go to a three-shift operation." The arbitrator required the employer to grant a paid lunch period to all employees when *some* employees were assigned to third shift, although the number of employees on third shift constituted only 4.5 percent of the total work force. Since the contract did not specify what constituted a three-shift operation, the company was deemed to be on a three-shift operation whenever it continued for a third shift work that had been done on a prior shift, regardless of the number of employees involved. (173)

In the above examples, the contract language was explicit and not amenable to being construed differently. In the following cases, the language was ambiguous.

Under the labor agreement at Conney-All Corporation a provision stated that "all employees shall be probationary employees during their first 45 working days of employment." Therefore, after having worked 43 full days and two half days on Saturdays, an employee was deemed to have completed his probationary period. Consequently he was entitled to the seniority date of his original hiring upon recall from layoff after less than one year. In interpreting "working day," arbitrator Samuel S. Kates ruled that the number of hours worked in any working day was unimportant; if it was a working day for the employee, it had to be counted as such whether he worked a full day or only part of a day. (174)

When is an employee an employee? That appears to have been answered, at least as far as Safeway Stores, Inc., was concerned. In a case there, an employee who was hired on the day before a holiday but who did not begin work until the day after the holiday was ruled to be "an employee" at the time of the holiday and was thus entitled to holiday pay. (175)

In this last example, the consequences could have been far-reaching, at least as far as the particular employer was concerned. The contract permitted a midterm reopening on wages only. It also provided that in the event no agreement was reached on an interim wage revision by a given date, the no-strike proviso was suspended until agreement was reached. The arbitrator interpreted this to mean that the entire contract, and not merely wages and the no-strike clause, was suspended in the event a strike occurred. To hold that employees might discontinue their services indefinitely, while contractual obligations on the company continued, would clearly be inequitable. Therefore, the employer was not liable for pay for a holiday that fell during the strike. (176)

PRIOR AWARDS AS PRECEDENTS

Is an arbitrator bound to follow the same doctrines that would ordinarily be applied by a court in considering earlier disputes and decisions of other tribunals? This question has been the source of continuing argument for many years. The very nature of the arbitration process, as it exists today, conceals from its own disciples a definite, specific answer. However, I will undertake to give some shape and form to the current state of the matter.

A 1950 study (177) of 528 arbitrators, companies, and unions, measured the weight it was thought the arbitrator should give precedents under other contracts. The findings are as follows:

Participant	Decisive Weight (%)	Some Weight (%)	No Weight (%)
Management	7	66	27
Union	19	59	22
Arbitrator	2	77	21
Average	7	70	23

If the above study is representative, a fairly reasonable assumption, it appears that the great majority of arbitrators are willing to give only "some weight" to prior awards. It then boils down to the question of what arbitrators consider to be "some weight."

It is generally agreed among arbitrators that arbitral opinions are not precedents, that each case stands upon its own feet. However, it also appears to be a well-established principle that the interpretation of contract language embodied in an award becomes a part of that contract language. This is a doctrine that is not seriously threatened even by those who protest against "citations" and "precedent." Until the parties change the labor agreement or until another arbitrator makes a contrary ruling, the interpretation of a contract is, in effect, part of the contract.

It can also be safely stated that arbitrators seldom give much notice to the legal discrimination among various types of precedents. The judicial doctrine of *res adjudicata* holds that a matter finally decided on its merits by a court having competent jurisdiction is not subject to litigation again between the same parties. The rule rests upon consideration of judicial time and public policy (factors not necessarily present in private arbitration hearings) favoring the establishment of certainty in legal relations. When a court has entered its final judgment on the merits of a cause of action, the parties are thereafter broadly bound, not only with regard to all matters considered by the court but also to any other admissible material that may have been offered, regardless of whether it was actually considered. The judgment of the court puts a practical end to the dispute, so that none of the adjunct issues can again be brought into litigation between the parties upon any ground whatever in the absence of fraud or some other overwhelming factor that would operate to invalidate the judgment. (178)

This does not pertain in the arbitration process. Arbitrators' awards do not have a corresponding authority or force. They are not accorded the weight of "judicial authority" in deterring future controversies—even between the same parties or over the same issues. Arbitrators do not consider prior awards conclusive or binding in subsequent cases. In arbitration, all questions of fact and law are deemed to be referred to the arbitrator for decision. Unless restricted by the contract, a submission agreement, or an applicable state statute, arbitrators do not bind themselves by strict rules of law or evidence. As long as he remains within his jurisdiction the arbitrator invariably feels free to decide the issues submitted to him, notwithstanding any prior awards between the parties.

What, then, is the "some weight" given by arbitrators to prior awards?

An examination of a large number of reported cases reveals that prior awards often do play a part in arbitration. However, instead of carrying the weight of "judicial authority," they exert a "persuasive" force that compels consideration. The extent to which this force is, in fact, persuasive and compelling in a given case is generally influenced by such questions as the following: (1) Is the present fact situation the same as the previous fact situation? (2) Are the same two parties who were involved in the past dispute involved in the present dispute? (3) Is the language of the labor agreement identical to that of the previous case? (4) If the same parties and the same labor agreement are involved, has a contract negotiation occurred during the intervening period, and, if so, were the contractual provisions changed? (5) Subsequent to a prior award, has a practice come into existence, mutually agreeable to the parties, which has the effect of modifying all or part of the prior award? (179) (6) Has another award been rendered which reverses or is contrary to the prior award? (7) Is the same evidence and argument involved in the present case, or is something new being presented that was not considered in the prior case? Finally, did the prior award evidence just and reasonable principles of conduct and contract interpretation?

One of the problems frequently encountered by arbitrators is the situation in which a party to an arbitration hearing presents citations of other published cases, presumably identical or very nearly so to its own, which, upon close examination by the arbitrator, prove to be dissimilar or unrelated. (180) Naturally, a party does not enhance its case when it does not exercise extreme care in its research and selection.

With reference to precedent, one is reminded of this story told by Erick Heller.

> A clown appears on a stage that is completely darkened except for a small circle of light cast by a street lamp in one corner. The clown, his face deeply worried and long-drawn, walks round and round the circle of light, obviously desperately looking for something.
>
> "What have you lost?" asks a policeman passing by.
>
> "The key to my house!"
>
> Whereupon the policeman joins in the search. Finding nothing after a while, the policeman inquires, "Are you certain you lost it here?"
>
> "No," replies the clown, and, pointing to the dark corner of the stage he says, "Over there."
>
> "Then why are you looking for it over here?"
>
> "Because there is no light over there," replies the clown. (181)

Obviously, if the parties want the arbitrator to find their precedential key, they must see that he looks in the right place.

When the particulars of a cited case are applicable to his own, an arbitrator may borrow its reasoning. In referring to a case cited by the union (182), arbitrator B. Meredith Reid stated: "With the reasoning there, as far as it went, your arbitrator agrees *and uses its principles* to state this Board finds as fact and *thus overrules that portion of the company's* position which claimed the grievants herein were 'temporary employees'; they were not" (emphasis added).

The relevance of previous awards made in disputes between the same parties to a present case is also determined by the similarity between the facts in the two cases. In the case of a company having a lot of trouble with light-bulb changing, the arbitrator in a prior case had ordered the company to pay an electrician call-out pay because a kiln operator had changed a light bulb. In the later case, arbitrator LeRoy Autrey denied a claim by another electrician for call-out pay because a maintenance mechanic had changed a light bulb. In the first case, the light bulb had been changed by an employee *not authorized* to handle electrical equipment. In the second instance, the maintenance mechanic *was so authorized.* Autrey disregarded the first award, since the bulb change did not require any high degree of skill, nor present any safety hazards. (183)

Where in a previous case good sense and reasoning has been shown after a fair hearing, arbitrators are cautious about rendering a new and different solution. (184) Carrying this principle one step forward, arbitrator Whitley P. McCoy came upon a situation in which he considered prior awards to have precedent value: "Where a number of competing companies negotiate jointly with a union, and agree on identical contract provisions in order to avoid competitive disadvantages, it would seem that the mutual intent of the several parties would be nullified if arbitrators should, by contradictory interpretations of the identical language, destroy the identity of the meaning." (185) So saying, McCoy ruled that, unless it was clearly wrong, a decision by one arbitrator under these circumstances should be followed by another. Having found that an earlier award had entitled salaried personnel to a full 40 hours' salary for any week in which they had worked at all under the given contract, he made the same ruling.

Despite protestations to the contrary, arbitrators have been known to "go along" with prior awards, *even those to which they do not wholly subscribe.* They have thus given them persuasive precedent value for the sake of stability and certainty between the parties in their contract interpretations. When serving on a special board of adjustment, Chairman Jacob Seidenberg expressed the opinion that had a given case been before him for the first time he might have decided otherwise; nevertheless he ruled that a pay dispute had to be resolved in accordance with prior awards on the same subject involving the same agreement. (186) In a similar case of greater complexity and wider-ranging implications, arbitrator Robert W. Fleming decided it was not important that he might have decided a prior case differently. The contract covered a number of plants all over the country. If he were to decide the dispute in a manner conflicting with the previous award, that would inevitably lead to other arbitrations of the same dispute in other plants. When it was brought out that the same facts had resulted in a decided dispute between another plant and another local of the union, but under the same national agreement, Fleming followed the previous awards and denied the grievance. (187) This is not to suggest that arbitrators will not reverse a fellow arbitrator when they feel he has erroneously interpreted a contract clause. (188) However, such reversals do appear to be exceptions to the generally followed rule of not disturbing "commonsense" prior rulings.

Although arbitrators usually minimize the importance of the precedent value of other awards, they do find sufficient merit in them to conduct their own research into how other arbitrators have ruled in similar cases. (189) On occasion they may even invite and encourage the parties to submit cited cases. (190)

As mentioned earlier, a factor affecting the weight given a prior award is whether a change has occurred in the contractual language since the previous award. Obviously, if one party or the other finds a particular award so objectionable as to be motivated to change the applicable contract language, and, in fact, is successful in collective bargaining negotiations, the same case brought forth a second time, under changed language, may understandably bring a different ruling, even before the same arbitrator. However, a small language change may not be enough. It has to be "sufficient to change the meaning." In an International Harvester case, the arbitrator found that a change had been made in the wording of the contract, purportedly in order to reverse the rule established by a prior award. In the final analysis it was insufficient to change the meaning of the earlier clause, and the arbitrator's award was in accord with the prior ruling. (191)

Arbitrators are also fairly consistent in giving substantial weight to prior awards where a negotiation has occurred since the previous ruling and the contractual language has not been changed. This specific point was emphasized by arbitrator Peter Seitz:

The Impartial Chairman is aware that the conflicting views as to whether the Turkus award applied to the handling of comics and rotos for suburban wholesalers and news companies were known to each of the parties at the time they were engaged in negotiations looking to the execution of a new Agreement. This conflict was not resolved in the negotiations. The Impartial Chairman is not disposed to regard the failure to do so as evidence of what the parties agreed to for the new contract term—but he is obliged to take this circumstance into consideration in determining what weight and effect to give to the Turkus award. *When they went into negotiation, they both knew that an arbitration award had been issued establishing a rule,* at the very minimum, affecting operations and overtime pay for direct delivery. Inasmuch as the same employees and crews in the same premises handle rotos and comics for both direct and indirect deliveries, *the Union was on notice that unless the Turkus Award, (whatever its scope) were changed in negotiations, in any subsequently held arbitration hearing involving the inextricably enmeshed operations for the handling of materials destined for indirect delivery, that the Turkus Award, necessarily would be given precedential weight.* [Emphasis added] (192)

All of the foregoing examples involved the ad hoc arbitral system. Obviously, one of the risks of that system is the possibility of conflict among the decisions of different arbitrators. Partly to minimize this danger, parties sometimes enter into contractual arrangements for permanent rather than ad hoc arbitrators. Under a permanent arbitration system, the likelihood of conflicting decisions is greatly reduced. The Chrysler-UAW arrangement is an excellent example of the permanent umpire alternative. The use of precedent in the Chrysler-UAW umpire system has been described as follows:

In every case the Chairman makes a careful review of all previous decisions that are indicated to be relevant to the matter at hand. Often his findings are rested in whole or in part on the principles enunciated in the earlier cases. Frequently, patterns and standards are evolved gradually on a case by case basis, with determinations being made on various aspects of a particular problem. Contract provisions once construed are uniformly applied, until such time as the parties themselves see fit to negotiate changes. Consistency of principles and their application is sought, not for its own sake, but as a matter of fairness and as an aid to promoting predictability at the arbitration step and workability in the parties' collective bargaining relationships. Thus, a body of case law is built up, and the system becomes institutionalized. The parties themselves recognize the precedent value of the decisions, not only in arbitration cases, but also on their day-to-day relationships. Although only two copies of a decision are issued to each side, both parties reproduce copies in large quantities and distribute them widely among officials and representatives of their organizations. For ready reference they supplement this by maintaining their own indexes and digests of cases. At the local levels, the parties attempt to make plant practices conform to principles announced in umpire decisions. There, they refer to decided cases in the working out of problems at the pre-grievance stage, or in the early steps of the grievance procedure. At the top levels, the decisions are almost always given immediate application in analogous disputes which may be, or come, before the (four man) appeal board. [193]

In summary, it can probably be safely said that in the usual ad hoc arbitration following precedent rests upon the assumption that the precedent has a sound and continuing validity. If a conflict in decisions results from a clear and supported conviction that the earlier decision would not reasonably resolve the issue, the arbitrator need not abdicate to his predecessor the function of judgment for which he was engaged. (194)

Although the doctrine of *stare decisis, et non quieta movere* (adhere to precedents, do not unsettle things) does not strictly apply to arbitration, the parties to a labor agreement value predictability of decisions and are reluctant to unsettle established matters.

Obviously, one of the primary purposes of the arbitral system is to aid the parties in reaching a clear understanding of their agreement as it applies to practice in the plant. Reopening decided issues, repeating attempts to persuade an arbitrator to change an established interpretation of the contract merely because one side or the other does not like it, or refusing to accept arbitral decisions as the basis for settling disputes without further arbitration, cannot fail to defeat this purpose. Arbitrators can and do make a positive contribution in this regard by laying a heavy burden of proof and persuasion on the party that claims a prior award was erroneous and should be reversed. This burden must clearly be heavier in cases involving the same contractual provisions as those in the previous case, the same facts, the same parties, and no new evidence or argument. Where such cases are faced, prior awards should be, and most often are, accorded persuasive value in the interest of stability of the decisional process.

PAST PRACTICE

The use of past practice to clarify ambiguities and to deal with a contract's generalities is commonplace among arbitrators. Arbitrators appraise the norms of conduct between the parties themselves to establish the intent of contract language that is susceptible to several interpretations, or vague or unclear. (195)

A clear contract probably allows those who administer it only one direction in their decision making. However, where the contract is silent or is susceptible to more than one interpretation (any one of which may be persuasively argued), management commonly fills in such gaps by exercising managerial discretion. Compounding this potential problem is the fact that the terms of the labor agreement are an umbrella over a number of operations, many of them perhaps diverse. The application of a common contractual provision to different operations and departments brings many management members into the decision-making process. Under these circumstances, it is not uncommon for them to find that they are not "singing out of the same hymnbook." Practices may vary from one section of the plant to another, one shift to another, or one supervisor to another. For this reason many employers attempt to insert a past-practice clause into the contract during bargaining. Representative of such a provision is the following:

> This Agreement supersedes all previous oral and written agreements between the company and the union. The parties do hereby cancel all past understandings, practices and customs. The parties herein agree that the relations between them shall be governed by the terms of this agreement only; no prior agreements, amendments, modifications, alterations, additions or changes, oral or written, shall be controlling or in any way affect the relations between the parties, or the wages and working conditions, unless and until such Agreement shall be reduced to writing and duly executed by both parties subsequent to the date of this agreement.

Management often seeks such a provision as a safeguard against a past-practice claim by the union. When the union submits a grievance that claims a continuation of a benefit or condition based on some alleged prior practice, management often cites such a past-practice clause to support its denial of the grievance and its rejection of the force of the alleged practice. Some companies have thereby escaped being encumbered with an undesirable practice when they were fortunate enough to have selected an arbitrator who endorsed this theory. In other cases, the defense was of no avail.

It is hard to identify standards by which arbitrators determine if there are practices that should be given some weight in their decisions. The more one investigates the many published decisions in which past practice was involved, the more it appears that there is no unanimity among arbitrators as to precise standards. The decision reached in any given case appears to depend largely upon the rationale of the arbitrator. Having said this, we will try nonetheless to sketch the sort of standards most frequently observed by the majority of arbitrators.

It appears that in the majority of arbitration decisions in which past practice or custom influenced the final outcome, the practices had one or more of the following characteristics. The more of these characteristics present in a case, the more weight accorded to the practice.

Unequivocality. The practice was granted or applied consistently, uniformly, regularly, and without break.

Clear acceptance. The practice was acquiesced in by the parties and was maintained without protest or objection from either.

Durability. The practice was followed over a reasonably long period of time. Some arbitrators attach significance to a practice commencing under one agreement and continuing unchanged and unprotested into a renewed agreement, bridging the collective bargaining negotiations between the parties without being changed or discontinued. It should also be noted that the *frequency* of the practice may not be as consequential as the *consistency* of its application. A practice that occurs only five times a year but is consistently and uniformly executed on each occasion may conceivably have more weight and effect than one occurring 15 times a year but inconsistently administered from one time to another.

Joint practice. Both parties through their line representatives operated as though the practice in fact existed and was a guiding example or rule. To some arbitrators this implies mutuality; the practice has resulted from bilateral as opposed to unilateral action. (196)

It is recommended that the practitioner who must determine if a practice in fact exists, ask the following questions: Has the practice been known to both parties and relied upon before in similar instances? How long has it existed? Has it extended over the term of more than one agreement? Are there any inconsistencies, contradictions, or deviations from the practice, and, if so, how materially contrary are the differences? Was the practice instituted bilaterally or unilaterally?

BARGAINING RECORD

Whenever a question arises about whether language changes have occurred or whether discussions have taken place in which a change of intent was agreed upon, the parties must turn to the negotiation records or to the participants themselves to fill in the void. Such research should provide answers to the following questions:

1. Is there a *new or changed* contract provision on the disputed matter?

2. If a *new* provision exists, which party proposed the language and what were the reasons for seeking a change? In this regard, which party's language was eventually adopted?

3. If the contractual provision has been changed from that appearing in the previous contract, who proposed the change and what were the reasons? Which party's proposal was finally adopted?

4. Were minutes of the negotiation meetings kept? What do they reveal about the discussions between the parties on the provision in dispute, irrespective of whether it is a new, a changed, or an unchanged clause?

5. Who represented management in these negotiations? Was he present during discussions on the relevant provisions? Is he available and able to supply credible accounts of what the parties intended?

6. Did either party attempt and fail to insert language in the contract to cover an uncovered subject?

Applying some of these questions to actual situations provides helpful insight into the significance of previous bargaining sessions. The arbitrator of a dispute between Anaconda Aluminum Company and the Aluminum Workers International Union stated:

After bargaining and discussions the parties in 1961 incorporated Article 28 into their collective bargaining agreement. This article relates to the contracting out of work. The article has been the subject of discussions in subsequent negotiations. A minor change has been made in it. In past negotiations the union has sought unsuccessfully to extend its restrictions to work sent out of the plant to outside contractors. *With this history of bargaining on the subject,* and within the meaning and spirit of the Fibreboard Decision (85 Sup. Ct. 398), there was no further obligation upon the company for additional consultation and bargaining with the union before the decision was made to subcontract the work in question. The evidence discloses that the union was given notice prior to the placing of the order. Under the fibreboard doctrine, once the parties have bargained in good faith on an issue and agreement has been rejected, there is no duty to bargain anew until the term of the contract expires or the parties mutually so desire. Once the bargain has been struck, interpretation and application of the agreement are called for, and not further bargaining. (197)

In another subcontracting dispute, the employer was held not to have violated the contract's recognition clause by subcontracting bagging work at a time when the bagging-room employees were on layoff. The contract did not include restriction on subcontracting, *and the union had been unsuccessful in negotiating such a limitation in the past.* Arbitrator A. Q. Sartain held that to have decided in favor of the union in this case would have been to give it through arbitration what it could not get through bargaining. (198) In a dispute at Food Employers' Council, Inc., arbitrator Thomas T. Roberts found a contract providing that "an employee shall be allowed three days funeral leave with full pay for death in the immediate family." He held that an employee whose father died while the employee was on vacation was not entitled to three days funeral leave or a three-day extension of his vacation. The ruling was based on the bargaining history, which indicated that at the time of their most recent negotiations both parties recognized that the funeral leave policy did not include payments of benefits during any period of paid absence from work, including vacations. (199)

Arbitrator Paul Prasow, in deciding a case for the Hitco Company and the Glass Bottle Blowers Association, made the following comments with regard to previous negotiations:

It was recognized during negotiations that there would be differences in the qualifications and availability of employees and the impossibility of absolutely equalizing overtime. Another subject of considerable discussion was the obligation of the company to train employees. *The union made a series of demands requiring the company to* train employees in connection with seniority, layoffs, and promotions. *At all times the company rejected such union demands and the contract contains no provisions in any section* where there is an obligation to train employees, in connection with seniority, layoffs, promotions, or overtime distribution. (200)

Examination of other arbitral decisions that were materially affected by the form and content of the bargaining sessions leads to certain generalizations, which may aid in answering the questions listed above. The party advocating a particular contractual provision appears to be required either to explain what it plans to gain by the clause or to phrase the provision in such a way that leaves no doubt before the subject is concluded. (201) One rule of particular importance holds that when the ambiguity is not removed by any other of the rules of contract construction and interpretation, the ambiguous and unclear contract language may be construed against the party who forwarded the proposal, (202) the reasoning being that the draftsman of the language can, by precision in phrasing, prevent any potential doubt as to its intended meaning. (203) However, it has also been held that ambiguous contract language need not be held or construed against the party who was its advocate, if there is no evidence that the other party has been confused by the ambiguity or misled as to its intent. (204) This concept, operating in reverse, was illustrated in a dispute at Safeway Stores, Inc.

The employer's alleged misleading assurances given during contract negotiations when the union's proposals to limit subcontracting and automation were rejected did not bar the employer's transfer of payroll and billing work from the bargaining unit to its electronic data-processing center. Material misrepresentations, if they had been established, might have constituted grounds for rescission of the contract, a circumstance which the union had not sought. However, in the absence of proof, the alleged assurances did not justify the imposition of obligations on the employer which could not be read into the contract as it stood. (205)

9

Evidence

STRICT observance of legal rules of evidence is not a common practice in the arbitration process. If required by both parties, the arbitration hearing will be conducted in this manner, but it is done infrequently. (206) Furthermore, many labor agreements mention the American Arbitration Association (AAA), either as the agency to be consulted in selecting the arbitrator or the one under the rules of which the process is to be conducted, or both. Rule 28 of AAA states: "The arbitrator shall be the judge of the relevancy and materiality of the evidence offered and conformity to legal rules of evidence shall not be necessary." (207)

Arbitrator W. Willard Wirtz, Secretary of Labor under Presidents Kennedy and Johnson, has made the following observation on this rather flexible subject: "Arbitrators have established the pattern of ordered informality; performing major surgery on the legal rules of evidence and procedure but retaining the good sense of these rules; greatly simplifying but not eliminating the hearsay and parole evidence rules; taking the rules for the admissability of evidence and remolding them into rules for weighing it; striking the fat but saving the heart of the practices of cross-examination, presumptions, burden of proof, and the like." (208) What this comes down to is that in the great majority of cases, "any evidence, information, or testimony is acceptable which is pertinent to the case and which help the arbitrator to understand and decide the problem before him." (209)

The practice of most arbitrators of allowing a liberal introduction of evidence has its share of critics, most of whom are members of the legal community. Lawyers have an instinctive aversion to the words of the arbitrator: "Well, I am not sure myself about its relevance [i.e., that of the alleged, evidence], but I will take it for what it is worth." However, Harry Shulman, late expert in arbitration, commented that "the more serious danger is not that the arbitrator will hear too much irrelevancy, but rather than he will not hear enough of the relevant." (210)

Arbitrator William E. Simkin, one-time national director of the Federal Mediation and Conciliation Service (FMCS), in commenting on the liberal acceptance of evidence, dwelt for a moment on the cathartic nature of such freedom:

> One of the fundamental purposes of an arbitration hearing is to let people get things off their chest, regardless of the decision. The arbitration proceeding is the opportunity for a third party, an outside party, to come in and act as a sort of father confessor to the parties, to let them get rid of their troubles, get them out in the open, and have a feeling of someone hearing their troubles. Because I believe so strongly that that is one of the fundamental purposes of arbitration, I don't think you ought to use any rules of evidence. You have to make up your own mind as to what is pertinent or not in the case. Lots of times I have let people talk for five minutes, when I knew all the time that they were talking it had absolutely nothing to do with the case—just completely foreign to it. But there was a fellow testifying, either as a worker or a company representative, who had something that was important for him to get rid of. It was a good time for him to get rid of it. (211)

The point is, of course, that, in the overwhelming majority of cases, arbitrators are receptive to almost any type of evidence the parties may wish to submit. What may not appear to be particularly germane at the outset may later be found intrinsic to the issue. Sometimes this can only be established as the case unfolds. It is a common practice for arbitrators to accept evidence "for what it is worth." This means that they are reserving their opinion of, and reactions to, the questionable evidence until they have had an opportunity to evaluate it against the record. Then, if in their judgment it is not sufficiently relevant to the issue at hand, they accord it no weight in their final determinations. (212) While it is true that some arbitration statutes require adherence to legal rules of evidence, the majority do not. (213) If no such requirement is made, or if it is general rather than specific and explicit, the strict observance of legal rules of evidence is customarily not necessary.

It would take an entire volume to provide a comprehensive treatment of the subject of evidence, so the remainder of this discussion will be concerned only with examples of the ways arbitrators commonly apply certain rules of evidence.

HEARSAY

Briefly, hearsay is something heard from another. "Hearsay evidence" is testimony that consists in a narration by one person of matters told him by another. Hearsay evidence is usually barred in legal proceedings because it cannot be tested through cross-examination. A written communication may also be categorized as "hearsay" and be equally as inadmissible as oral testimony; the fact that a hearsay statement is reduced to writing does not render it admissible. Obviously, it is as impossible to cross-examine a written document as it is an absent third party.

Generally speaking, arbitrators also reject hearsay evidence when it is properly objected to. The reasons are self-evident—the contesting party has no chance to confront or cross-examine the alleged witness. Hearsay testimony may be motivated by self-interest, malice, or spite. It may be the misrepresentation of an irresponsible person or it may be partially or totally fabricated.

Inasmuch as arbitrators do not consider themselves bound by strict legal rules of evidence, they tend to admit hearsay evidence and weigh it in the light of the lack of opportunity to cross-examine. For example, arbitrator Harold I. Elbert has ruled that doctors' certificates are admissible in an arbitration proceeding as proof of an employee's illness although they may be hearsay. (214) An examination of reported arbitration decisions indicates that medical certificates are commonly admitted in evidence and given weight by arbitrators in determining whether an employee was sick. (215)

The observations of arbitrator Benjamin Aaron on the weight to be accorded hearsay evidence is well worth consideration:

> A competent arbitrator may be depended upon substantially to discount some kinds of hearsay evidence that he has admitted over objection. He will do so selectively, however, and not on the assumption that hearsay evidence, as such, is not to be credited. If, for example, a newly appointed personnel manager, or a recently elected business agent, offers a letter to his predecessor from a third party, the arbitrator is likely to ignore the fact that the evidence is hearsay; if satisfied that the document is genuine, he will give it such weight as its relevancy dictates. On the other hand, hearsay testimony about statements allegedly made by "the boys in the shop" or by executives "in the front office," though perhaps not excluded from the record by the arbitrator, probably will have no effect on his decision. (216)

Another arbitrator, Arthur R. Lewis, has commented that "the reasons calling for the existence of a hearsay rule in common-law jury actions should at least guide the judgment of the arbitrator in the evaluation of the weight, if any, to be attributed to such evidence in an arbitration proceeding." (217) In any case, it is extremely unlikely that an arbitrator will decide an issue with a ruling based on and supported by hearsay evidence alone. (218) It is worth noting that the rules of AAA allow the arbitrator to receive and give consideration to the evidence of witnesses by written document, but recommend that it should be given only the weight to which it is deemed to be entitled after consideration of any objection made regarding its admission. (219)

CIRCUMSTANTIAL EVIDENCE

Circumstantial evidence is regarded with caution by arbitrators, just as it is by the courts. To be decisive such evidence should preclude any reasonable theory or hypothesis other than that which it purports to establish. Such evidence, frequently given in arbitration proceedings, is generally resorted to in the absence of any direct proof of the fact at issue. It consists of a number of peripheral events or conditions that, taken together, reasonably point to the fact.

At the Stockham Pipe Fitting Company, circumstantial evidence was sufficiently persuasive to uphold a discharge action in a dispute over the discharge of employees for instigating an unauthorized work stoppage. Arbiter Whitley P. McCoy decided the matter and evaluated the web of circumstances surrounding it:

> Because of the secret nature of the offense of these men, proof is extremely difficult. It does not follow from this that proof may be dispensed with or that mere suspicious circumstances may take the place of proof, as I have indicated in sustaining the grievances of four men. But I think it does follow that something less than the most direct and the most positive proof is sufficient; in other words, that, just as in cases of fraud and conspiracy, legitimate inferences may be drawn from such circumstances as a prior knowledge of the time set for the strike. Unusual actions in circulating among the employees just prior to 9:30, communication of the time set to employees, and signals however surreptitious, given at that hour. Mere prior guilty knowledge of the time set would not alone be sufficient since presumably many of the employees must have been told the time a half-hour, an hour, or several hours in advance. Nor would merely being the first in a department to quit at the stroke of 9:30, standing alone be sufficient. A wave of the hand, which might as reasonably be interpreted as a signal of goodbye as a signal to others to go out, as in the case of Hollingsworth, would of itself be insufficient. But these or other suspicious circumstances, in combination, and especially in case of known leaders in the Union's affairs, may be sufficient to convince the reasonable mind of guilt. (220)

The opinion of the majority of arbitrators is that circumstantial evidence is real evidence, providing every other possible explanation is eliminated. However, where too many imponderables remain, the doubt is resolved in the grievant's favor. Long experience has also taught that circumstantial evidence may in fact be more persuasive than the direct evidence in certain cases. However, arbitrators remain understandably cautious.

In deciding a dispute between the Illinois Bell Telephone Company and the International Brotherhood of Electrical Workers, arbitrator Meyer S. Ryder discussed the standards of proof to be used when circumstantial evidence is involved:

> The Chairman holds that in discharge matters where the employee offense being treated with carries along with it connotations of

corruption and illegality, were the employee to be held guilty of the offense, the standard of evidentiary proof to convict should be no real subjective question of guilt in the minds of him or those who have to decide. Acceptable to this proposition should be evidence of circumstances or combination of circumstances such as leave no doubt that what is indicated is actually present. Should it be considered that the application of standards of proof in a criminal proceeding under the law go beyond and are greater than these standards, then the criminal law standards should not be held to apply in an industrial relations arbitration proceeding. Accordingly, the Chairman has applied the standards he has enunciated above to the discharge matters. (221)

Arbitrator Paul M. Herbert has commented that the use of circumstantial evidence "does not eliminate in any sense the requirement that there must be a clear and convincing proof to establish that the offense charged was committed." (222) It has also been said that mere suspicion is not sufficient to establish a wrongdoing. (223)

Putting it still another way, arbitrator Clair V. Duff has stated: "[The arbitrator] must exercise extreme care so that by due deliberation and careful judgment he may avoid making hasty or false deductions. If the evidence producing the chain of circumstances pointing to guilt is weak and inconclusive, no probability of fact may be inferred from the combined circumstances." (224)

OFFERS OF COMPROMISE

The purpose of the contractual grievance machinery is to provide an instrument by which the parties may seek and, hopefully, find remedies to problems between them. To maintain its functional purpose, such machinery must be by the parties in an open and uninhibited way. If their mutual interests and needs are to be served, each party must feel free to search for accommodation or negotiate compromises. Each must be free of fear that if its offers are refused they will not subsequently be interpreted as a sign of weakness by an arbitrator.

For this reason, arbitrators give very little weight, if any at all, to revelations of previous offers. (225) The logic of this attitude is sound. One arbitrator put it succinctly: "It is clear that any offer made by either party during the course of conciliation cannot prejudice that party's case when the case comes to arbitration. It is the very essence of conciliation that compromise proposals will go further than a party may consider itself bound to go on a strict interpretation of its rights." (226)

The following is an example of this same concept in action. Upon returning to work after a back injury, an employee had refused, on the advice of the union, to consult yet another doctor, after having submitted to examinations by the employer's doctor and a clinic. Arbitrator John Sembower ruled that that evidence had to be disregarded. The arbitration was dealing with a dispute involving the employer's refusal to reinstate the employee. It appeared to Sembower that the final medical examination was part of an attempt to settle the grievance before arbitrating it. As such, he held that the parties' attempts to resolve their differences should not be allowed to prejudice their positions at arbitration. (227)

If proposals, counterproposals, and offers of compromise could be seized upon and used later in arbitration against a party, the result would be a throttling and stifling of the dispute-settling efficiency of the grievance machinery. Consequently, it is rarely allowed.

DISCIPLINE CASES

Management must stand ready to support its allegations against employees charged with improper conduct. What this means when such an issue is brought to arbitration is that the party bearing the burden of proof will be required to open the case and present its position first and will also be given the right to close the hearing with a position statement. Of course, this procedure may be altered or waived.

It seems to be a well-established tenent of labor relations that the burden of proof in disputes over discipline or discharge must be carried by the party "holding the affirmative"—that is, the party initiating the action. *The employer* is therefore called upon to establish the facts it asserts as the basis for having taken positive corrective action.

Arbitrators differ in the quantity and quality of proof demanded of the employer. Some require that guilt be established "beyond reasonable doubt," as in the criminal courts. Labor arbitrators are inclined to impose this standard when the charges are by nature criminal or involve substantial injury to the employee's work status, job security, or reputation. (228) To others, the burden of proof is carried if a "preponderance of the evidence" establishes a prima facie case. In such an instance, the burden of proof may actually be transferred from one party to the other during the arbitration proceedings.

Various arbitral opinions can be quoted to demonstrate these alternative requirements for supplying proper and adequate proof. Representative of the "preponderance" view is this comment by arbitrator Harry H. Platt: "In a case of discharge the burden of proof rests upon the company to show, by a fair preponderance of the evidence, that the discharge of an employee was for good and sufficient cause." (229)

It is probably safe to say that most managements will argue for "a preponderance of the evidence" measurement. On the other hand, some arbitrators adopt the "beyond reasonable doubt" standard of proof applied in criminal law. Arbitrator Robert J. Wagner put it this way: "In the discharge of two employees with over 12 and 13 years' service respectively, it would seem to be the responsibility of management to show beyond a reasonable doubt that the employees are unable to perform a fair day's work." (230)

Arbitrators are not in complete accord on the extent to which the rules of evidence and procedure applicable to criminal law should be used in disputes over accusations of moral turpitude. A reading of many cases involving such issues creates a definite impression that a majority of arbitrators require proof beyond a reasonable doubt. (231) An explanation of this philosophy was well articulated by arbitrator James V. Altieri in settling a dispute between the Publishers Association of New York City and the New York Stereotypers Union over the discharge of an employee for willful damage to company property:

> The union cites a long array of awards holding that in cases of this kind the proof should be beyond a reasonable doubt. In the field of proper industrial relations, the philosophy is as valid as in either sociological and jurisprudential relationships, that it is better for an occasional guilty person to escape unpunished than to court the possibility, through less exacting norms, not only of punishing employees with loss of their jobs for acts of which they may not be

> guilty but (of placing) . . . upon them what might be an insur-
> mountable burden in getting other employments. (232)

Clearly, in this view, management has an obligation not to discipline or discharge employees unless its expectations are reasonable and it has conducted an adequate and objective investigation
to establish proof of the guilt of anyone accused of wrongdoing.

Finally, the credibility of witnesses weighs more heavily in the
balance then does their number. One should not be deluded into
thinking that the more witnesses called to repeat a circumstance,
whether a discipline case or any other, the more credible the arbitrator will find the information. As a matter of fact, it is quite
possible for him to believe the party with fewer witnesses if the
testimony seems sounder. (233) It should also be realized that the
failure of a disciplined or discharged employee to take the stand
in his own defense cannot be considered as evidence or presump-
tion of guilt. (234)

BEST EVIDENCE

The wisest rule is always to use the best evidence available. As
an obvious example, eyewitness accounts will certainly provide
more compelling testimony than will hearsay. If challenged, a
supervisor's testimony that an employee was not at work, will be
considered more conclusive if it is supported by payroll and production records and other such evidence.

Arbitrators look askance at testimony or evidence introduced
by the employer about events that occur after a discharge action.
In determining whether the action taken by the company fits the
accusation against the employee, arbitrators are concerned only
with the employees' conduct preceding the discharge.

It is unwise to hold back records and information germane to
the grievance issue. If time cards, production records, absenteeism
reports, payroll records, prior grievance or arbitration settlements, and the like are available and related to the case, they
should be introduced. To be of maximum effectiveness, such information should have been discussed and/or presented and made
available to the other party preceding the arbitration hearing, preferably during the earlier stages of the grievance procedure.

Occasionally, disputes have come up between the parties not

only because of the company's failure to supply pertinent information, but also because of its refusal to provide relevant evidence. In a case between North American Aviation and the United Automobile Workers, the company acknowledged that supervisors had improperly performed work belonging to unit employees, and it agreed to reimburse the employees who had thereby been deprived of work. However, it refused to furnish the union with the names of the employees reimbursed or the amounts paid to each of them. This refusal resulted in another grievance. The arbitrator rejected the company's position and ruled that the union's right to such information was "part and parcel of its role of collective bargaining agent." (235)

In cases involving charges of violation of the National Labor Relations Act, it has been held, even in cases in which there were no contract provisions to aid the union, that:

a. An employer is required to furnish a union on request with sufficient data on wages and allied matters. (236)
b. This requirement includes original data on time studies. (237)
c. The data must be furnished for the processing of grievances as well as for general collective bargaining. (238)
d. As to relevance, it is sufficient if the information sought is "related" to the issue. (239)
e. Such data must be supplied even though the employer considers it confidential. (240)

There is danger inherent in arbitrary refusals of information requested by the union. There are additional reasons why supplying information and placing it on the record, so to speak, is desirable. Under some agreements, it may even be essential that such information be forwarded if it is to be considered appropriately admissible at the arbitration hearing. For example, a rather typical contractual clause reads:

> The arbitrator shall arrive at his decision solely upon the facts, evidence and contentions as presented by the parties during the arbitration proceeding.
>
> The arbitrator shall not consider any evidence which was not introduced by the parties in the steps of the grievance procedure as set forth herein, unless such evidence was not then known to the parties, and also unless the parties mutually agree to the presentation of such evidence.

A survey conducted by arbitrator W. Willard Wirtz indicated that "unless some deliberate attempt to mislead the other party is disclosed, and particularly if the 'new' evidence or argument appears substantially material, most arbitrators will be disinclined to rule the matter out of the proceedings." (241) In the contractual clause above, the absence of any provision prohibiting the introduction of new evidence may persuade the arbitrator to receive evidence that is being presented for the first time at the hearing. (242)

Court rules are designed to exclude evidence that is irrelevant but might impress an unsophisticated jury. When a judge hears a case without a jury, he is supposed to know enough to disregard the irrelevant. Arbitrators are looked on in the same light. A court will not upset an award on the ground that the arbitrator admitted bad evidence, or even on the ground that he was influenced by it.

Expert testimony is admissible—and an arbitrator will rarely make it as difficult for an expert to qualify as a court would. In addition, if the case involves a confession of some sort, it is unwise to suppress part of it.

The primary evidence important in discipline and discharge cases consists of the following matters:

a. The employee's previous work record.
b. The clarity of the foreman's instructions.
c. The presence of any provocation for the act leading to discharge not attributable to the employer.
d. The absence of any provocation for the act leading to discharge attributable to the employer.
e. The reasonableness of any order that was issued and disregarded.
f. The existence of and employee-union knowledge of an established rule governing the misconduct.
g. Any reasons for misunderstanding or confusion.
h. The presence of eyewitnesses to the incident.
i. The penalties meted out to others for similar offenses.
j. The established fact that the employee charged is the one who breached a rule.

These are not intended to include all the factors involved in each and every dispute; but they will be found to be applicable in the majority of instances.

No documentary evidence may be submitted until after the other party has first examined it, or has waived its right to do so.

LIE-DETECTOR TESTS

Employers seem to be using lie detectors increasingly, particularly in industrial discharge cases. For some time, an argument has been boiling in labor-management circles about the relevance of the polygraph test and its admissibility as evidence in arbitration hearings. Employers not only use its results as evidence of the guilt of a discharged employee, but also regard an employee's unwillingness to submit to the test as indicative of guilt.

This controversy is probably an outgrowth of the dispute over the use of polygraph tests in criminal proceedings. The *Manual for Prosecuting Attorneys* states the reasons for which the tests are not usually admitted an evidence by the courts: "Such tests have not yet gained such standing and scientific recommendation among physiological and psychological authorities as would justify the courts in admitting expert testimony deduced from the discovery and development and experiments thus far made." (243)

A number of trial courts have allowed the testimony of lie-detector examiners in instances in which counsel for both sides had agreed to the test before it was given and had stipulated that the examiner's interpretation could be used in evidence without objection from the party adversely affected by it. Presumably, these conditions could make the tests admissible in arbitration proceedings as well. A reading of the published awards on this issue shows that arbitrators generally deny consideration of the results of lie-detector examinations. (244)

Judge Norman N. Eiger ruled in an arbitration proceeding that he could not, in view of the majority position of the courts of the land, determine the rights of an individual according to the results of a lie-detector test. He stated: "The arbitrator holds that these tests . . . have no probative value and are not admissible as evidence in these proceedings." (245)

Arbitrator Albert A. Epstein commented somewhat more cautiously on the use of polygraph tests, but his decision was nonetheless the same:

> The use of the test has been the subject matter of much discussion in both court proceedings and arbitrations. There is no clear law or practice in this area. It is argued that there is always the possibility that the tests are not accurate and that the emotional state or condition of the individual being tested may affect the validity of

the test. There is enough of a conflict among scientific authority and legal and arbitrative precedents to warrant a serious doubt about the probative value of the polygraph test. (246)

The closest one can come to an arbitral decision that accords with the use of lie-detector tests is the finding in a case between Westinghouse Electric Corporation and the I.U.E. The employer had imposed disciplinary suspensions on three wildcat strikers who were involved in assaulting a car containing another employee. During the processing of the grievances, both the grievants and their victim agreed to take polygraph tests, with the understanding that the results would be disclosed to the company and the union and would be made available to any party for the purpose of resolving the grievance. At the arbitration hearing later, arbitrator A. T. Singletary permitted the admission of the test results. Although he did not pass upon the reliability of the report of the polygraph examinations, he did observe that the conclusions reached in it were corroborated by the conclusions he drew from other evidence. (247)

The qualifications of the individual conducting the lie-detector testing are often in question. For example, at Spiegel, Inc., the results of a lie-detector test given to an employee suspected of stealing were not allowed as evidence by arbitrator John Sembower because the operator of the lie detector was not considered qualified to verify test results. First, the arbiter considered the operator's training and educational background to be meager. Second, under cross-examination by the employer's counsel, the operator professed recognition of nonexistent works and authors in the polygraph field. (248)

Another discharge, motivated in part by the results of a polygraph test administered to the fired employee, was set aside by arbiter Daniel Kornblum because of the polygraph's unreliability as proof of guilt. (249)

What happens when an employee refuses to submit to a polygraph test? In a case at Town and Country Food Company, the arbitrator found that a discharge for alleged insubordination was not justified on the basis of a refusal to take a lie-detector test. (250) Arbitrator Meyer S. Ryder commented: "However, where there is employee refusal to give consent to such testing, the refusal, standing by itself and coupled or not coupled with the presence of factual material giving reasonable suspicion of culpability, is not that kind of behavior that should be an offense in and of itself. To punish for refusing to consent on the basis that this is lack of cooperation appears to supply an overtone of being required to self-incriminate, a proposition repugnant to Anglo-Saxon legal codes." (251)

10

The Remaining Parts of Your Case

A FAMILIAR anecdote will illustrate the situation of many representatives who become oversold on the virtues and merits of their own cases. A passerby watching a sandlot baseball game between two youthful teams inquired of the catcher, "What's the score?"

"Sixty-six to nuthin'," was the reply.

"It looks bad for you fellows, doesn't it?"

"Oh, I dunno. Our side hasn't been up to bat yet."

Such an attitude occurs too often among advocates in arbitration proceedings. Confidence and optimism are essential qualities in this endeavor, as in any other, but it is unwise to ignore one's technical or evidentiary deficiencies. Not to anticipate the presentation, arguments, evidence, and case theory of one's adversary may leave gaping holes in one's own case structure.

A hearing will run for several hours or several days, depending on how complicated the problem is. Though in some cases it would be possible to state both the evidence and the arguments in writing, a hearing enables the parties to adapt their presentation to what the arbitrator seems to need: specifically, to answer each other immediately and in terms suited to the occasion. Similarly, the arbitrator counts on oral exchanges between the parties to give him the feel of the situation and to clear up many details that would be overlooked in written presentations. If there are conflicting witnesses, he can try to judge their credibility from their demeanor, as well as asking them questions to obtain more information.

An advocate should try to present his case as clearly and fully as possible, without relying on the arbitrator to bring out important points. In presenting facts, he should state the conclusions that he draws from them, and that he thinks the arbitrator should draw as well.

A hearing should be dispensed with only if the issue is quite clear and the facts well established—preferably by a written statement to which both the company and the union have agreed.

Hearings are usually private. Attendance is limited to the arbitrator, representatives of the parties, and the counsel and witnesses required. The union side sometimes includes a shop committee. If management, the union, and the arbitrator consent, visitors may also be admitted; reporters rarely are. Under the rules of the American Arbitration Association, the arbitrator can decide on the admission of persons who have no direct interest in the case. Occasionally a union will ask that the hearing be open to its members as a means of educating them in the problems of union leadership. This is usually permissible so long as the spectators do not in any way interfere with the proceedings.

The parties may be and sometimes are represented by counsel. As a rule, if a party desires to be so represented, he is required to notify the other parties within a reasonable time before the hearing is held. Under the American Arbitration Association's rules, if arbitration is initiated by counsel to the other party, or reply is made by counsel, notice is deemed to have been given. In most cases, some skill in marshalling evidence and preparing briefs is necessary to the effective presentation of a case. This is not to say that the advocate must be legally trained or educated, but only that whatever his education he should possess a basic understanding of evidence and procedure, a disciplined mind, and an ability to organize and correlate a variety of facts and information. He must also be articulate, mentally alert, and quick to perceive developments at the hearing table as they may unexpectedly evolve. Occasionally, when a technical point or question is involved, a specialist such as a time-study engineer or some other technician with intimate knowledge of the situation can be effective in presenting information as a witness. Sometimes members of the labor relations staff become experts at presenting arbitration cases; they are likely to be most familiar with the issue, perhaps having previously dealt with it in the grievance or negotiation stages.

PROCEDURAL DON'TS

In an excellent article entitled "Some Procedural Problems in Arbitration," Benjamin Aaron made these pertinent remarks on the subject of what not to do in arbitration.

> By far the greatest number of procedural problems arising in ad hoc labor arbitration concern the introduction of evidence and the examination of witnesses. These are problems, too, which seem to bring out in some attorneys those irritating qualities that comprise the average layman's stereotype of the lawyer. A few of the more unpleasant of these traits may be mentioned in passing. First, by a wide margin, is the use of legal mumbo-jumbo: the monotonous objection to the introduction of evidence on grounds that it is "incompetent, irrelevant and immaterial," or "not part of the res gestae." A close second is the eat-em alive method of cross-examination: the interrogation of each witness as if he were a Jack the Ripper finally brought to the bar of justice. Last, but scarcely least, there is the affectation of what may be called advance documentship: throwing an exhibit at one's opponent across the table, as if contamination would result if it were handed over in the normal way, or contemptuously referring to the opponents' exhibits as "pieces of paper that purport to be," and so forth. These tactics may be well suited to stage or cinema portrayals of the district-attorney-with-a-mind-like-a-steel-trap or the foxy defense counsel at work, but they are wholly out of place in an arbitration proceeding. Moreover, they can be counted upon almost invariably to exacerbate the feelings of those on the other side and to initiate bitter and time-consuming arguments between the parties. (252)

While Mr. Aaron has touched upon some very real mistakes often made by advocates in the arbitral process, there are still others which need to be avoided because they are likely to injure one's case:

- Reliance on a minimum of facts and a maximum of argument.
- Withholding essential facts or not telling the whole truth or resorting to trickiness or distortion of facts.

- Overemphasis, or exaggeration of the grievance or charge.
- Lack of supporting evidence such as documents or records, or unwillingness to produce them, or refusal to let the impartial arbitrator personally examine them.
- Introducing recalcitrant witnesses who create antagonism.
- Trying to put a lay arbitrator at a disadvantage by introducing legal technicalities.
- Giving the impression of overfriendliness or secret influence with the arbitrator.
- Bickering with the other party across the table.
- Showing lack of cooperation with the arbitrator or disrespect for him.
- Calling witnesses whose testimony merely duplicates what has been given, unless denial by the other party makes this necessary.

The advocate should try to *balance quality and quantity* of testimony. He should offer no more than is necessary to convince the arbitrator. He should avoid far-fetched arguments, or the arbitrator will conclude that his case is weak. He should not introduce facts regarding the other party's previous attempts to compromise the issue. The case should not be closed until he is satisfied that all of his facts, evidence, and argument are fully on the record. If he feels that the submission of a post-hearing brief is in his party's best interest, he should not close the hearing until he has discussed with the arbitrator and the other party, jointly, the procedure for mailing and exchanging such briefs.

WITNESSES

It is fairly customary to make witnesses swear an oath to tell the truth. But this is perhaps a needless formality. If a person is determined to tell the truth, the oath is a superfluous ritual. If, on the other hand, he is motivated not to tell the truth, the oath will not be much of a deterrent. Moreover, the arbitration hearing is merely a quasijudicial proceeding and there is no penalty for lying or perjury. If a stenographic record is kept, however, this may have a steadying effect.

Witnesses are usually seated around the table, and are called upon as the case proceeds. Sometimes a witness may be requested to leave the room while another person's testimony is being given.

For most witnesses, appearing at an arbitration hearing is a new experience, and they become nervous or anxious over it. The prospective witness fears that he may look foolish and embarrass himself before his friends and associates. He knows he will be subjected to cross-examination by someone who may be skillful enough to make him contradict himself, even though he intends to tell only the truth as he knows it.

The following suggestions are addressed to prospective witnesses to help them discharge their task as ably and effectively as possible.

- Assume a fairly erect but comfortable position in the witness chair. This will enable you to sit without fidgeting. A witness who is constantly shifting about may seem to lack credibility, particularly during cross-examination.
- Remember that the arbitrator is the man who must be convinced—not the opposing counsel.
- Do not argue with the opposing counsel, or be sarcastic, or get angry, or try to outwit him.
- Tell the truth. If part of your testimony is not favorable to your party, it is the responsibility of your advocate to cope with that.
- Be alert and attentive. Keep your mind on the business at hand.
- Watch the arbitrator, particularly if he is taking notes, and particularly if no stenographic record is being made. Remember that if you talk too fast he may miss certain details that can be helpful to your case. Adjust your pace to his writing speed, if possible.
- If the arbitrator asks you questions, answer as directly as you can. Do not be overly friendly.
- Carefully consider every question. There is no need to answer immediately. Reflect for a moment. Do not let the other party's counsel set the pace for your responses.
- Do not be afraid to answer, "I don't know." No one is presumed to have an answer to all questions.
- If you do not understand a question, ask the counsel if he will please repeat it. Do so as many times as are required for you to comprehend the question. If you answer without being certain what is sought, you may guess wrong and supply an answer that is misunderstood by the arbitrator, who has not interpreted the question the same way.

- Do not volunteer information to the other party's counsel. Answer his questions honestly but directly, and with a yes or no if possible. If there is something left unsaid by you which could be helpful to your case, it is the responsibility of your party's counsel to bring it out during re-direct examination.
- If the other party's counsel asks you if you have discussed your testimony with your counsel, reply that you have, since this of course is the truth. If he asks you whether you were told what to say, reply that you were not—that you were told simply to tell the truth.
- Be sure to tell your counsel *all* you know relevant to the case— particularly anything that may be actually or potentially damaging to your side. Counsel cannot cope with damaging information unless he is informed of it. He should not be surprised by it at the hearing.
- Be prepared to swear an oath to tell the truth.
- While you are being cross-examined, if your counsel objects to a question, or a procedure, or a piece of evidence, keep silent. Do not insist on going ahead and answering. The objection may be valid; it may have been made simply to upset the opposing counsel; or it may have been made to give you a breather and a chance to think about what you have been saying. Your counsel is in charge of the case, and you must follow his lead.
- Be neatly groomed.
- Use whatever notes, letters, memos, diaries, or receipts you may have to aid your memory and lend credibility to your testimony, but be sure to review them first with your counsel.
- Do not mumble. Speak clearly and forthrightly, but not aggressively. Keep your hands away from your mouth.
- If you need to visit the rest room, speak up and request a brief recess.
- If your hear testimony from someone else that reminds you of something you had forgotten, or if you know such other testimony to be false or misleading, pass a note quietly to your counsel advising him of this.

If the hearing brings out new facts or considerations that favor one side, the counsel for that party may consider asking for a recess to discuss possible settlement with the other party. If the other party agrees, both sides may welcome a chance to cut short a long hearing. The maneuver is more likely to be successful if the parties have been bargaining with each other long enough to be used to the process of give and take, and do not feel that they lose face by one defeat or compromise.

THE MOVING PARTY

In all but discipline cases, the union is the moving party, the one asserting a claim, and it should make at least a preliminary or introductory presentation. In most cases, the union is expected to go ahead and present its whole case before the company does so. In an arbitration proceeding, the party with the substantive burden of proof, usually the union as the complaining party, has the task of presenting the initial evidence. The union must establish that a contract violation has occurred. If it establishes what is called a prima facie case (defined as support of the complainant's contentions by evidence, that, if believed, would sustain those contentions), the employer must rebut that evidence.

The substantive burden of proof—whether in a court of law, in an arbitration proceeding, or in a grievance processing—rests with the complaining party. As we have said, in most cases the complaining party is the union. However, it seems a well-established tenet of labor relations that the burden of proof in disputes over discipline or discharge must be carried by the party holding the affirmative of the issue—that is, the party who initiated the challenged action; the employer is, therefore, called on to establish the facts it asserts as the basis for having taken presumably positive corrective action. In such cases the employer must open the case and present its position first, and it will also be given the right to close the hearing with a position statement. This procedure may of course be altered or waived by agreement of the parties.

11

Representative Arbitral Conclusions
—Critical Issues

THE ARBITRATOR usually hands down his award either within a stipulated time after the close of the hearing, or within a stipulated period after the receipt of briefs. The time limit may even be specified in the contract. It may also be specified in the assigning panel's rules, or in an applicable state law. The award must be in writing and signed. It may or may not be accompanied by an opinion in which the arbitrator sets forth the reasoning by which he arrived at the award.

Some arbitrators feel that it is unwise to accompany the award with a written opinion because the opinion itself may become a source of wrangling; arbitrators' awards do, however, tend to become a body of precedent supplementing the basic contracts from which they grow.

To be effective, the award should meet the following requirements:

- It should involve no further hearings or future action by the arbitrator after the award is made.
- It should reserve to the arbitrator no powers or duties extending beyond the date of signing the award.

- It should not go beyond the terms of the arbitration agreement —i.e., it should settle only the issue submitted.
- It should observe all conditions set forth in the arbitration agreement.
- It should be rendered within the time limits, if any, set forth in the agreement, or, if the agreement is silent on this point, in the rules of the arbitrating agency.
- It should be certain and definite in its terms and so phrased that it is possible of performance.
- It should be accompanied by a well-reasoned opinion.

This brings us to certain key issues which are often critical for parties contemplating arbitration. They are selected on two bases: they represent issues that are the most troublesome when they arise; and they illustrate certain well-established generalizations with which parties facing arbitration should be quite familiar, and which have been accepted and handed down from one arbitrator to another.

SUBCONTRACTING

For the sake of brevity, this discussion excludes contracts expressly defining the company's authority to contract out. Contracts with such express provisions generally either limit management's contracting-out prerogatives, or expressly provide management with an unhindered right (253) What follows is concerned with the more elusive subject of *implied* limitations, and with how arbitrators wrestle with this issue. (254)

When the contract is silent and contains no explicit language to bar the company from sending work to subcontractors, there may be one or a combination of several clauses that can be construed as implying an intention to limit contracting out. These include the recognition clause; the seniority clause; and the list of job classifications.

The recognition clause is the provision that most frequently captures the fancy of arbitrators who search for implied reasons to limit management's contracting-out prerogatives.

Perhaps the most complete answer to those who seek erroneously to find an implied agreement or limitation in the recognition clause (255) was given by Professor Herman Gray, when he stated:

> In my view, the purpose of the Recognition Clause is no more than to enunciate the legal status of the bargaining union. It describes the unit of the employees for whom the Union speaks and thus delineates the operative scope of the agreement itself. It serves no substantive function. That is, it does not deal with and has no bearing upon the terms and conditions governing the employment itself. To read substantive provisions into the Recognition Clause through arbitration decisions is, in my judgment, to use arbitration as a means for expanding the agreement which the parties have made, rather than just interpreting and applying its provisions in specific situations. (256)

The seniority clause has given rise to similar interpretations with respect to contracting out. On the surface it merely establishes a preference for longer service employees over shorter service employees when the amount of work available is limited. Since such a clause provides that shorter service employees will be laid off before the others, it obviously recognizes that the volume of work can diminish. (257) Arbitrator Saul Wallen has said:

> In the same way the seniority provisions guarantee, not a constant employment opportunity for each category of employees covered by the contract, but a set of rules for the parcelling out of employment opportunities, the availability of work can be affected by diminished work volumes due to changes in the market, due to changes in technology, or due to changes in the realm of good faith managerial decision-making. (258)

As to those arbitrators who refuse to imply restrictions, what do they use as a basis for their awards? Basically, they take the simple, straightforward view that management has reserved the right to contract out, unless, by specific contract language, this right has been limited. But most of them apply certain standards to evaluate the propriety of the subcontract action. (259) Some of the standards are listed below. These are not intended to be all-inclusive. They are merely some which have, singly or in combination, been decisive in certain cases.

* *The effect on the union.* Was the subcontracting done to injure or discriminate against the union, and did it substantially prejudice the status of the unit? (260)

- *The availability of qualified employees.* Was the skill possessed by available members of the unit adequate to perform the required work, and are such employees readily available in the numbers needed? (261)
- *The availability of facilities and equipment.* Were equipment and facilities currently available, and, if not, could they have been readily and economically acquired? (262)
- *Duration and regularity.* Was the contracting-out for a temporary or permanent period, and was it done frequently or spasmodically? (263)
- *Negotiation history.* Has the subject been discussed in negotiations, and has the union made demands to limit the right to subcontract? (264)
- *Past practice.* Has work been contracted out in the past, and to what extent? (265)
- *Type of work.* Has the work contracted out customarily been done by unit employees? Was the contracting-out done for economy or security? Was it an emergency or special job, or was it done to augment the regular work force? (266)
- *The effect on the unit.* Did the contracting-out action displace or lay off employees, or cost them regular or overtime earnings? (267)

These are the yardsticks most often applied in contesting a contracting-out action when the labor agreement does not provide specific language on the subject. (268)

DEMOTION

A majority of arbitrators, but a small one, frown on demotion as a form of discipline in the absence of a specific contractual provision authorizing such a penalty. The contrary view is that management has retained its right to use demotion for disciplinary purposes unless the agreement expressly limits its right to do so.

The reasons for thinking demotion an improper penalty are numerous. In demoting an employee, management imposes a penalty of indefinite duration. The action can affect the seniority rights not only of the penalized worker but of others, who become unintended victims. It can weaken the demoted employee's job security by making him more vulnerable to layoff. It may jeopardize his ability to obtain more meaningful and profitable positions in the future. It is too often the easy or less troublesome way out of a situation that calls for discharge or some other form of discipline. It may also be discriminatory: one worker may be demoted three labor grades while another, guilty of the same offense, may be demoted two or four. Demotion should be related to the employee's competence and qualifications, not to breaches of plant rules, which call for discipline.

If an employee has the ability to perform a job, and is withholding his ability, this is a condition subject to correction through progressive discipline. The reason for the behavior is irrelevant. Whether it arises from a misplaced sense of independence, from work group pressures, or from circumstances in his private life, his behavior is unjustified so long as it is within his control.

A case involving the Bethlehem Steel Company illustrates this point. The arbitrator held that management's demotion of an employee was improper because his record indicated that he had the requisite ability for the job, stating that disciplinary action rather than demotion was the proper remedy where substandard performance was found to be temporary. (269) The two significant facts are that the employee possessed ability and that he had demonstrated it previously. His failure at his task was merely temporary.

The arbitrator of another dispute held that the Boeing Company could demote an employee who was not capable of performing the work, but was not entitled to demote an employee when the evidence showed that his errors were the result of negligence rather than inability. (270) Similarly, an arbitrator deciding a case involving the Republic Steel Corporation rules that it could not use demotion as a form of discipline for occasional carelessness or for failure to obey instructions on the job. (271)

MANAGEMENT RIGHTS

Employers commonly practice a residual rights theory of management. The residual rights theory holds that the employer retains the residue of all rights it has not bargained away; all rights not bargained away continue to reside in management.

The preponderance of arbitral opinion holds the following view of the employer's residual rights: "It is now a well established generalization that every employer continues to have all powers previously had or exercised by employers unless such powers have been curtailed or eliminated by statute or by contract with a union. . . ." (272)

While this is generally true and fairly typical of the concept endorsed by the overwhelming majority of arbitrators, there are some exceptions. If a contract is silent on a particular subject, this does not necessarily mean that the subject is automatically left to management's discretion. Therefore, disputes which arise over matters not covered by pertinent contract language will not always be resolved in the company's favor. The customs and practices of the parties during the term of the agreement, and perhaps during previous agreements as well, may constitute a significant or even controlling factor in an arbitrator's final decision.

QUITTING VERSUS CONSTRUCTIVE DISCHARGE

While some authorities equate a discharge to any termination of employment (273), most experts (and modern arbitral opinion almost universally so holds) limit discharge under collective bargaining agreements to a termination due to some failure of the employee. (274)

It is fundamental that an employee can voluntarily quit his employment, and it is obvious that he may do so without explicitly announcing his intention—for example, by deliberately acting in a manner that justifies his immediate termination. However, he must have the *intention* to sever himself from his employer; otherwise, his conduct cannot be properly characterized as quitting. An employee of the Wood Newspaper Machinery Corporation had been hired to work in the engine lathe department. He had on occasion been transferred to the turret lathe department, which he did not like. After his latest assignment, he requested transfer back to the engine lathe department. When this was not given him after a month, he demanded immediate transfer saying that otherwise he would resign. Shortly thereafter, despite the suggestion of the company and the union committee that he defer action until the return of the business agent, he resigned. The union contended that the resignation was forced by the company's unreasonable and discriminatory refusal to transfer him. The paramount initial question in this case was whether the termination of employment was voluntary or brought about by some action or fault of the company. Arbitrator Emanuel Stein ruled that when he resigned instead of filing a grievance, he engaged in a voluntary act. (275) This is typical of many other decisions in similar cases. (276)

A more common situation is that in which a supervisor directs an employee to do a certain task, giving him the option of either obeying or being deemed a quit. The view taken by the great majority of arbitrators is that expressed by Howard S. Bellman:

> If the Company can, without prior agreement with the Union, determine that certain employee conduct, other than voluntary and intentional abandonment of employment, constitutes quitting, it can thereby avoid the aforementioned restrictions (just cause proof). An employee thought to have been insubordinate may be warned and subsequently discharged. The employee and the union, in turn, may challenge the company's action as without "just cause" and receive an impartial determination as to its propriety. But were the company able to effectively assert to the employee, "if you refuse to work as you are ordered, you will have quit," the company could preclude the impartial application of the "just cause" standard as well as any necessity to warn the employee (as this contract required).
>
> Therefore, the Company's contention that X quit simply because the company proposed to him that if he did not work as assigned he would be quitting, is rejected. Also rejected is the general proposition that leaving work rather than accepting an assignment amounts to quitting. (277)

This issue has been arbitrated many times. The consistent and uniform holding has been that an individual is deemed to have quit *only* when his conduct and words demonstrate a clear and deliberate intent to quit.

VIOLATION OF NO-STRIKE PLEDGE

In the overwhelming majority of cases, workers observe the no-strike clause. Arbitrators usually sustain disciplinary action taken by companies against those workers guilty of striking in violation of the no-strike promise.

The issue before the arbitrator in disputes over company action against strikers is usually whether the employer was arbitrary or discriminatory in his selection of those to be disciplined or discharged. Arbitrators have usually ruled that a company cannot single out an individual striker for discipline or for heavier punishment unless it can prove that he was a leader of the strike. (278)

Whether participation in a wildcat strike justifies the company's denying strikers all the protective provisions of the contract is an unsettled question among arbitrators. Some have ruled that workers terminated their service under the contract by participating in an illegal strike. (279) One concluded that violation of the no-strike article did not terminate the contract and that participants did not cease to be employees. (280) Another held that an employer was free to ignore the seniority and recall provisions of the contract when resuming operations after such a strike, when no claim was made that the recall process adopted was discriminatory. (281)

If union officials have participated in a wildcat strike, a harsher penalty will generally be upheld on the premise that this is a graver offense for them than for the ordinary employee. (282) Not only must union officials refrain from engaging in "negative leadership"; some arbitrators hold that they have an obligation, by virtue of their union position, to demonstrate "affirmative leadership" in opposition to contractual violations by employees. (283)

In the majority of cases in which arbitrators modified or reversed a company's action toward participants in wildcat strikes and slowdowns, the reason given was that the evidence was inadequate, the penalty too severe, or that the company was discriminating against particular strikers.

A careful study has shown that in this area the proportion of disciplinary actions upheld by arbitrators is about the same as in others, while the proportion of outright reversals is possibly the lowest of any major class of dereliction. (284)

DISCIPLINE AND DISCHARGE

It seems to be a well-established rule of contract administration as handed down in the great majority of arbitral opinions that an employer does not have an unrestricted right to discipline, even though the collective bargaining agreement does not expressly and specifically limit it. In other words, the mere presence of a labor agreement tends to require the employer to show cause for any disciplinary action. The reasoning is that a fundamental purpose of the agreement is to provide the workers with some form of job security. To allow an employer to exercise solely his own discretion in determining the justness of his discipline and discharge actions would render this promise null. (285)

Discharge and discipline continue to be the issues most frequently submitted to arbitration.

Arbitrator Carroll R. Daughterty has developed seven criteria that he has applied in a number of published decisions on discipline cases. His stature as an arbitrator makes these standards noteworthy.

1. Did the employee have foreknowledge that his conduct would be subject to discipline, including possible discharge?
2. Was the rule he violated reasonably related to the safe, efficient, and orderly operation of the company's business?
3. Did the company make a reasonable effort before disciplining him to discover whether he in fact did violate this rule?
4. Was its investigation fair and objective?
5. Did it obtain substantial evidence that the employee was guilty of the offense with which he was charged?
6. Was its decision nondiscriminatory?
7. Was the degree of discipline given him reasonably related to the seriousness of his proven offense and/or to his record with the company? (286)

The majority of arbitral decisions have held that even when a contract contains no general limitation on management's rights to discharge, a just cause restriction is implied. (287)

Arbitrators differ as to the quantity and quality of proof they demand from the employer. Some require that guilt be established "beyond reasonable doubt," as in a criminal court. Arbitrators are inclined to impose this standard when the charges are by nature criminal or involve substantial injury to the employee's work status, job security, or reputation. (288) Others see the burden of proof as carried if a "preponderance of the evidence" establishes a prima facie case. Under this criterion, the burden of proof may actually transfer from one party to the other during the arbitration proceedings. (289)

Although parties to labor agreements today enjoy a higher level of sophistication than at any time in the past 30 years, discharge and discipline are still too frequently at issue in arbitration cases. An analysis of the many hundreds of published cases on these subjects suggests that management and labor still have a long way to go before they achieve a satisfactory understanding of their mutual rights and responsibilities.

Conclusion

THE PROCESS of arbitration is thriving today. Each year the proportion of grievances resolved in the terminal stages of the arbitral processes grows. One of life's eternal conflicts is that between the effort of every man to get the most he can for his services and that of society—in the form of the employer—to get his services for as little as it can. Combination on the one side is patent and powerful. Combination on the other is the necessary and desirable counterpart, if the battle is to be carried on in a fair and equal way. One of the manifestations of this constant struggle is the raising of complaints and grievances that often lead to an impasse between the parties. The method almost universally employed for the resolution of such stalemates, wherever there is a collective bargaining agreement, is arbitration by a neutral person. When the system works fairly well, its value is great. Arbitration is an integral part of the system of self-government. The system is designed to aid management in its quest to preserve essential management prerogatives, and it is also designed to aid unions in their quest for a sense of participation in the decisions governing the enterprise. It is also designed to provide employees with an assurance that they will receive a full measure of industrial justice.

An agreement to arbitrate constitutes a surrender of a company's right to determine the controversy by unilateral action or by voluntary agreement or by a test of economic strength. It likewise constitutes a surrender of the union's right to test its contentions by a show of economic strength. In the field of industrial relations, arbitration is the substitution of reason for the struggle of opposing forces.

Arbitration, therefore, should not be approached as a battleground but rather as a peaceful, cooperative arrangement for the determination of matters upon which the parties have honestly failed to agree.

Voluntary arbitration is a safeguard of the free enterprise system in that its successful use will forestall governmental interference in the affairs of labor and management. It is a procedure for the fostering of good will and mutual understanding. Labor and management have a common interest in preserving it.

Citations

Abbreviations

ARB   *Labor Arbitration Awards,* published by Commerce Clearing House, Chicago.

BNA   Bureau of National Affairs, Washington.

LA   *Labor Arbitration,* published by the Bureau of National Affairs, Washington.

LRRM *Labor Relations Reference Manual,* published by the Bureau of National Affairs, Washington.

Citations to the three journals listed above take the following form: citation number; journal number; abbreviation of journal name; page number, e.g., 10. 46 LRRM 80.

1. Taylor, George W. "Preface to Frieden," *Labor Arbitration and the Courts.* BNA, 1952.
2. Shulman, Harry. "Reason, Contract and Law in Labor Relations." *Harvard Law Review* 68 (1955): 999–1024, reprinted in *Management Rights and the Arbitration Process.* BNA, 1956.
3. Jaffé, Louis L. "Labor Arbitration and the Individual Worker." *The Annals of the American Academy of Political and Social Science,* May 1953, pp. 40–41.

4. Maginis v. Panhandle Pipe Line Co., 23 LA (1954): 570.

5. Frieden and Ulman. "Arbitration and the War Labor Boards." *Harvard Law Review* 58 (1945): 309.

6. The Bureau of National Affairs. *Contract Clause Finder; Collective Bargaining—Negotiations and Contracts.* BNA, 1970.

7. Coulson, Robert. "Labor Arbitration: The Insecure Profession." *Proceedings of NYU Twentieth Annual Conference on Labor.* Albany, N.Y.: Mathew Bender & Co., 1967.

8. Westerkamp, Patrick R. and Miller, Allen K. "The Acceptability of Inexperienced Arbitrator: An Experiment." *Labor Law Journal,* December 1971.

9. The proceedings of the National Academy of Arbitrators are published annually in book form by the Bureau of National Affairs (BNA). The following volumes are now available from the publisher:

   - *The Profession of Labor Arbitration: Selected papers from the First Seven Annual Meetings of the NAA* (1948–54).
   - *Arbitration Today: Proceedings of the Eighth Annual Meeting* (1955).
   - *Management Rights and the Arbitration Process: Proceedings of the Ninth Annual Meeting* (1956).
   - *Critical Issues in Labor Arbitration: Proceedings of the Tenth Annual Meeting* (1957).
   - *The Arbitrator and the Parties: Proceedings of the Eleventh Annual Meeting* (1958).
   - *Arbitration and the Law: Proceedings of the Twelfth Annual Meeting* (1959).
   - *Challenges to Arbitration: Proceedings of the Thirteenth Annual Meeting* (1960).
   - *Arbitration and Public Policy: Proceedings of the Fourteenth Annual Meeting* (1961).
   - *Collective Bargaining and the Arbitrator's Role: Proceedings of the Fifteenth Annual Meeting* (1962).
   - *Labor Arbitration and Industrial Change: Proceedings of the Sixteenth Annual Meeting* (1963).
   - *Labor Arbitration—Perspectives and Problems: Proceedings of the Seventeenth Annual Meeting* (1964).
   - *Proceedings of the Eighteenth Annual Meeting* (1965).
   - *Problems of proof in Arbitration: Proceedings of the Nineteenth Annual Meeting* (1966).
   - *The Arbitrator, the NLRB, and the Courts: Proceedings of the Twentieth Annual Meeting* (1967).

- *Developments in American and Foreign Arbitration: Proceedings of the Twenty-first Annual Meeting* (1968).
- *Proceedings of the Twenty-Second Annual Meeting* (1969).
- *Arbitration and Social Change: Proceedings of the Twenty-Second Annual Meeting, National Academy of Arbitrators* (1970).

10. 46 LRRM 80.

11. Dravo-Doyle Co. and International Union of Operating Engineers' Labor Agreement, 1969.

12. Labor Agreement between Union Carbide Corp., Nuclear Division, and Atomic Trades and Labor Council.

13. Labor Agreement between General Dynamics Corp., Convair Division, and the International Association of Machinists, 1960.

14. Labor Agreement between City of New York Board of Education and United Federation of Teachers, 1970.

15. 33 LA 802—Arsenault v. General Electric (Connecticut Supreme Court); 34 LA 39—Calka v. Tobin Packing Co. (New York Appellate Division); 31 LA 240—Hearst Corp. (New York Supreme Court).

16. Pond Lily Co. and Textile Workers (United Textile Workers of America, 1966.

17. Labor Agreement between Brunswick Corp. and Local Lodge 1813, International Association of Machinists, 1972.

18. 34 LA 39—Calka v. Tobin Packing Co. (New York Appellate Division).

19. Labor Agreement between Abex Corp., S. K. Wellman Division, and Mechanics Educational Society, 1970.

20. Labor Agreement between Englehard Minerals and Chemicals Corp. and Local 238, United Cement, Lime & Gypsum Workers International Union, Gardner, Ga., 1972.

21. Labor Agreement between the Boeing Co. and International Association of Machinists, effective Dec. 12, 1971.

22. Labor Agreement between McDonnell Douglas Corp. and International Association of Machinists, 1972.

23. Sherwood Medical Industries, Inc. and District 50, United Mine Workers, 1969.

24. Labor Agreement between American Enka Corp. and United Textile Workers of America, 1969.

25. 26 LA 122—Babylon Milk and Cream Co. v. Horvitz (New York Supreme Court, 1956).

26. Stein, Emanuel. "Problem Areas in Labor Arbitration." *New York University Third Annual Conference on Labor,* pp. 167–86. Albany, N.Y.: Mathew Bender & Co., 1950.

27. Labor Agreement between Brunswick Corp. and the United Brotherhood of Carpenters and Joiners, Local 824, 1972.

28. Bureau of National Affairs. *Basic Patterns in Union Contracts, No. 397.* BNA, 1969.

29. Labor Agreement between Local Lodge 1813, International Association of Machinists, and Brunswick Corp., 1972.

30. See 42 LA 623.

31. See 41 LA 871 and 54 LRRM 2598.

32. See 43 LA 431 and 57 LRRM 2125.

33. See 41 LA 257.

34. U.S. Department of Labor. *Bulletin #908–16.* Washington: U.S. Government Printing Office, 1969.

35. See 46 LRRM 2414.

36. See 46 LRRM 2416.

37. Bureau of National Affairs. "Annual Labor Contracts Survey." *Collective Bargaining Negotiations and Contracts.* BNA, 1969.

38. See 14 LA 953.

39. See 39 LRRM 2524.

40. Labor Agreement between Broadway-Hale Stores Inc. and Retail and Wholesale Department Store Union (RWDSU).

41. See 48 LRRM 2967.

42. Labor Agreement between United Brotherhood of Carpenters and Joiners of America, Local 824, and Brunswick Corporation, 1972.

43. Baer, Walter E. *Grievance Handling: 101 Guides for Supervisors.* New York: American Management Association, 1970.

44. See 31 LA 494.

45. See 32 LA 228.

46. See also 33 LA 374; 34 LA 643; 34 LA 814.

47. See 35 LA 330.

48. See 44 LA 624.

49. Bureau of Labor Statistics. "Grievance Procedures: Major Collective Bargaining Agreements." *Bulletin No. 1425–1.* Washington: U.S. Dept. of Labor, November 1964.

50. Labor Agreement between Olin Mathieson Chemical Corp. and the International Association of Machinists, 1968.

51. See 34 LA 306.

52.   See 45 LA 707.

53.   See 44 LA 545.

54.   See 33 LA 847.

55.   See 42 LA 376.

56.   See 42 LA 988.

57.   See 34 LA 102.

58.   See 35 LA 237.

59.   West Texas Utility Co. v. NLRB, 346 U.S. 855 (1953); Hughes Tool Co. v. NLRB, 503 (Court of Appeals, Fifth Circuit, 1945); NLRB v. North American Aviation, Inc., 656 (Court of Appeals, Ninth Circuit, 1943).

60.   See 41 LA 947.

61.   See 42 LA 376.

62.   See 41 LA 966.

63.   See 43 LA 140.

64.   For a complete volume covering the entire scope of past practice see Baer, Walter E.   *Practice and Precedent in Labor Relations.* Lexington, Mass.: Lexington Books, D.C. Heath & Co., 1972.

65.   See 3 LA 840; 24 LA 295; 26 LA 393.

66.   See 33 LA 553; 25 LA 534.

67.   See 4 LA 170; 9 LA 595; 31 LA 959.

68.   Labor Agreement between Local Lodge 1813, International Association of Machinists, and the Brunswick Corporation, 1966.

69.   See 41 LA 406.

70.   See 42 LA 854.

71.   See 44 LA 574.

72.   See 32 LA 704.

73.   See 43 LA 16.

74.   Elkouri, F., and Elkouri, E.   *How Arbitration Works.* BNA, 1960.

75.   See 45 LA 275.

76.   *Collective Bargaining and Negotiating Contracts.* BNA, 1970.

77.   See 48 LA 496.

78.   Labor Agreement between General Analine and Film Corp. and International Chemical Workers.

79.   Labor Agreement between Lockheed Aircraft Corp. and the Engineers and Scientists Guild. (Ind.), 1966.

80.   See 44 LA 878.

81.   See 42 LA 153.

82. See 45 LA 1000.

83. See 42 LA 470.

84. See 37 LA 794; 15 LA 207; 18 LA 662; 23 LA 21; 20 LA 416; 24 LA 141; 26 LA 501.

85. See 43 LA 1126.

86. See 42 LA 1247.

87. See 44 LA 304.

88. See 5 LA 175.

89. See 31 LA 917.

90. See 10 LA 664.

91. See 43 LA 129.

92. See 44 LA 156.

93. Bureau of National Affairs. *Basic Patterns in Union Contracts, No. 648.* BNA, April 2, 1970.

94. Labor Agreement between Associated Spring Corp., Bristol Div., and the United Auto Workers, 1964.

95. See 42 LA 153.

96. See 45 LA 225.

97. See 58 LRRM 2593 (44 LA 448).

98. The Bureau of National Affairs reports that 96 percent of the labor agreements in 1966 contained no-strike clauses.

99. Drake Bakeries, Inc. v. Local 50, American Bakery and Confectionary Workers, 370 U.S. 254; 45 LA 17, 676 (1962).

100. See 60 LRRM, 2222; 59 LRRM 2745; 57 LRRM 2528; 58 LRRM 2344.

101. See 57 LRRM 2521.

102. See 59 LRRM 2341.

103. Commons, John R., and Andrews, John B.   *Principles of Labor Legislation,* p. 430. 4th rev. ed. New York: Harper and Bros., 1936.

104. Webb, Sidney, and Webb, Beatrice.   *Industrial Democracy,* p. 241. London: Longmans, Green and Company, 1919.

105. "Mediation, Investigation, and Arbitration in Industrial Disputes," quoted in Howard S. Kaltenborn. *Governmental Adjustments of Labor Disputes,* p. 218. Chicago: Foundation Press, 1943.

106. Report prepared by an Independent Study Group, published by the Committee for Economic Development, 711 Fifth Ave., New York, 1961, p. 109.

107. Maggiolo, Walter.   "Mediation's Role on the Labor Stage." *Labor Law Journal* 4 (1953): 658.

108. Commons and Andrews, *Principles of Labor Legislation,* p. 430.

109. U.S. Department of Labor. *First Annual Report of the Secretary of Labor, 1913*, p. 9. Washington: U.S. Government Printing Office, 1914.

110. U.S. Department of Labor. *Second Annual Report of the Secretary of Labor: Fiscal Year ended June 30, 1914*, p. 21. Washington: U.S. Government Printing Office, 1914.

111. Bureau of National Affairs. *War Labor Reports: Reports of Decisions of the National War Labor Board with Headnotes and Index-Digest*, vol. 1. Cited: 1 War Labor Report. BNA, 1942.

112. Ibid. (105).

113. National Labor Relations Board. *Legislative History of the Labor Management Relations Act, 1947*, vol. 2, p. 1145. Washington: U.S. Government Printing Office, 1948.

114. Ibid., vol. 1, p. 300.

115. Ibid., vol. 2, p. 1654.

116. U.S. Congress. "Labor Management Relations Act," 1947, *Title II—Conciliation of Labor Disputes in Industries Affecting Commerce; National Emergencies*, sec. 203, (b). Washington: U.S. Government Printing Office, 1947.

117. Peter Seitz. "The Mediator, who he is, what he does, and how to use him" and "People at Work: the Human Element in Modern Business: Some Principles and Practices in Industrial Human Relations." *AMA Management Report No. 1*, pp. 91 and 165. New York: American Mangement Association, 1957.

118. Federal Mediation and Conciliation Service. *Facts Behind the Headlines in Labor-Management Disputes*, p. 5. Washington: U.S. Government Printing Office, 1961.

119. Meyer, Arthur S. "Function of the Mediator in Collective Bargaining." *Industrial and Labor Relations Review* 13 (January 1960) 161.

120. Bureau of National Affairs. *Management Rights and the Arbitration Process: Proceedings of the Ninth Annual Meeting of the National Academy of Arbitrators.* BNA, 1956.

121. See 37 LA 335.

122. Bureau of National Affairs. *Collective Bargaining—Negotiations and Contents, No. 397.* BNA, 1969.

123. Labor Agreement between National Dress Mfrs. Assn. and International Ladies' Garment Workers Union, 1966.

124. Labor Agreement between Gulf Oil Corp. Port Arthur Refinery and Oil, Chemical and Atomic Workers Union, 1970.

125. Labor Agreement between Coleman Company, Inc. and Tool Craftsmen Independent Union, 1966.

126. Ibid., (citation no. 100).

127. John Wiley and Sons v. Livingston, 376 U.S. 543, 555 (1964).

128. United Steelworkers v. Enterprise Wheel and Car Corp., 363 U.S. 593, 597 (1960).

129. For these criteria and a full coverage of the subject, see Herbert Schmerty. *When and Where Issue of Arbitrability Can be Raised.* Englewood Cliffs, N.J.: Prentice-Hall, Inc. 1966.

130. For this and other coverage see "Procedural Arbitrability—A Question for Court of Arbitrator?" *Labor Law Journal.* December 1963, p. 1010.

131. See no. 130.

132. See 24 LA 761.

133. See 34 LA 617; 33 LA 777; 28 LA 659.

134. See 28 LA 321.

135. See 46 LA 473.

136. See 46 LA 369.

137. See 33 LA 130.

138. See 33 LA 390.

139. See no. 127.

140. See 25 LA 39.

141. See LA 878.

142. See 1 LA 215.

143. See 25 LA 50.

144. See 21 LA 502.

145. See 22 LA 456.

146. Labor Agreement between International Harvester Co. and United Auto Workers, 1964.

147. See 22 LA 456.

148. See 19 LA 737 and also 15 LA 474.

149. Jules Justin. *Arbitrability and the Arbitrator's Jurisdiction: Management Rights and the Arbitration Process.* BNA, 1956.

150. See 34 LA 288; also see 12 LA 230; 10 LA 480; 5 LA 410; 7 LA 767.

151. See 29 LA 469.

152. See 42 LA 376.

153. See 44 LA 10.

154. See Smith v. Bowen, 121 N.E. 814 (Mass. 1919); and Reichart v. Quindazzi, 6 N.U.S. 2d 284 (N.Y. 1938).

155. See 1 ARB 67,012.

156. See 25 LA 94.

157. See 21 LA 129.

158. See 29 LA 188.

159. See 31 LA 82.

160. See 33 LA 825.

161. See 15 LA 46.

162. Butte Water Company v. Butte, 138, p. 195 (Mont. 1914)

163. See 10 LA 227.

164. See 5 LA 753.

165. See 29 LA 188.

166. See 22 LA 769.

167. See 21 LA 139.

168. See 12 American Jurisprudence, 227, p. 746.

169. See 6 LA 838.

170. See 13 LA 110 and 24 LA 715.

171. See 31 LA 634.

172. See 44 LA 196.

173. See 21 LA 679.

174. See 41 LA 169.

175. See 22 LA 466.

176. See 24 LA 560.

177. Warren, Edgar L., and Bernstein, Irving. *A Profile of Labor Arbitration.* BNA (238 responding arbitrators), 1966.

178. See Von Moschzisker. *Res Adjudicata, 38 Yale Law Journal* 299 (1929); *Symposium on Res Adjudicata, 39 Iowa Law Review* 213 (1954).

179. See 25 LA 426.

180. See 24 LA 193; 32 LA 247; 25 LA 126; 22 LA 181; 16 LA 74; 22 LA 336.

181. Heller, Erick. "Oswald Spengler and the Predicament of the Historical Inauguration." *The Disinherited Mind,* p. 181–97. New York: Farrar, Straus and Cudahy, 1957.

182. See 25 LA 149.

183. See 63–1 ARB 8063.

184. See 62–2 ARB 8611; 62–2 ARB 8584; 63–2 ARB 8695; and also 11 LA 945; 25 LA 896; 37 LA 830.

185. See 62–3 ARB 8882.

186. See 62–3 ARB 8946; also 39 LA 567; 28 LA 476.

187. See 62–3 ARB 89641 and 33 LA 25.

188. See 24 LA 379; also 9 LA 761.

189. See 16 LA 111; 16 LA 844; 32 LA 126; 32 LA 156.

190. See 15 LA 934.

191. See 16 LA 217.

192. See 32 LA 360.

193. Wolff, David A.; Crane, Louis A.; and Cole, Howard A. "The Chrysler–UAW Umpire System." *Proceedings of the Eleventh Annual Meeting—National Academy of Arbitrators.* BNA, 1958.

194. See 9 LA 757.

195. For a full coverage of this subject see Baer, Walter E. *Practice and Precedent in Labor Relations.* Lexington, Mass.: Lexington Books, D.C. Heath & Co., 1972.

196. For examples of the arbitral application of these factors see 28 LA 439; 28 LA 14; 29 LA 372; 3 LA 137; 3 LA 760; 29 LA 256.

197. See 48 LA 409.

198. See 44 LA 102; also 41 LA 165; 45 LA 184.

199. See 45 LA 291.

200. See 47 LA 726.

201. See 17 LA 63 and 21 LA 196.

202. See 11 LA 228; 21 LA 196; 2 LA 399; 8 LA 452.

203. See 11 LA 228.

204. See 13 LA 133.

205. See 42 LA 353.

206. See 10 LA 955.

207. See 30 LA 1086.

208. Wirtz, Willard W. "Due Process of Arbitration." *The Arbitrator and the Parties* 1, 13. BNA, 1958.

209. Simkin William, and Kennedy, William. *Arbitration of Grievances, Bulletin No. 82,* p. 25. Washington: U.S. Department of Labor, Division of Labor Standards, 1946.

210. Shulman. "Reason, Contract, and Law in Labor Relations." *Harvard Law Review* 68 (1955): 999, 1017.

211. *Conference on Training of Law Students in Labor Relations, vol. 3, Transcript of Proceedings. Harvard Law Review* (1947): 636–37.

212. See 16 LA 32.

213. See 10 LA 955.

214. See 42 LA 583.

215. See 29 LA 291; 20 LA 451; 19 LA 417.

216. Aaron, Benjamen. "Some Procedural Problems in Arbitration." *Vanderbilt Law Review* 10 (1957): 733–44.

217. See 16 LA 727.

218. See 19 LA 571; 8 LA 518; 20 LA 880.

219. See 30 LA 1086; Rule 29.

220. See 4 LA 744; 7 LA 239.

221. See 39 LA 470; 45 LA 490; 40 LA 598.

222. See 29 LA 604.

223. See 19 LA 413.

224. See 29 LA 718.

225. See 24 LA 430.

226. See 8 LA 993.

227. See 41 LA 591.

228. See 39 LA 352; 29 LA 272; 24 LA 804.

229. See 1 LA 254.

230. See 7 LA 147.

231. See 42 LA 803.

232. See 43 LA 400.

233. See Pawnee v. Farmers Elevator and Supply Co., 76 Colo. 1 and 227 P. 2d 836.

234. For full coverage of the subject of discipline cases, see Baer, Walter E. *Discipline and Discharge Under the Labor Agreement.* New York: American Management Association, 1972.

235. See 17 LA 121.

236. See *Labor Relations Expediter,* Collective Bargaining, Sec. 19. Compare NLRB v. Truitt Mfg. Co., 351 U.S. 149, 38 LRRM 2042 (1956).

237. See 31 LRRM 1334 and 33 LRRM 2129.

238. See 25 LRRM 1475 and 33 LRRM 2461.

239. See 36 LRRM 2220; 35 LRRM 2215; 35 LRRM 2730; 27 LRRM 2524.

240. See 10 LRRM 49; 11 LRRM 693; 3 LRRM 2220.

241. Wirtz, Willard W. "Due Process of Arbitration." *The Arbitrator and the Parties,* p. 15. BNA, 1958; and 17 LA 183.

242. See 17 LA 183 and 1 ARB-67, 327 (1946).

243. New York University. *Practicing Law Institute,* 1959, 492.

244. See Fleming, Robbert. "The Polygraph and the Arbitration

Process." *Michigan Law Review* 60 (1961): 12; reprinted as *Reprint Series No. 111.* Urbana: University of Illinois, Institute of Labor and Industrial Relations, 1969.

245.   See 38 LA 778.

246.   See 45 LA 1155.

247.   See 43 LA 450.

248.   See 44 LA 405.

249.   See 44 LA 709.

250.   See 32 LA 44.

251.   See 39 LA 470.

252.   Institute of Industrial Relations. *Reprint No. 67.* Los Angeles: University of California, Los Angeles, 1957.

253.   See Crawford, Donald. *Challenges to Arbitration: Proceedings of the Thirteenth Annual Meeting of National Academy of Arbitrators,* pp. 52–53. BNA, 1960.

254.   See 14 LA 31.

255.   See 30 LA 851; and Slichter, Sumner H., et al. *The Impact of Collective Bargaining on Management.* Washington: The Brookings Institution, 1960; and 22 LA 251. Also see 13 LA 991, 24 LA 158, 35 LA 397.

256.   See 26 LA 723.

257.   See 19 LA 503, 20 LA 432.

258.   See 28 LA 491.

259.   See 19 LA 219, 27 LA 174, 28 LA 270, 29 LA 594, 28 LA 491.

260.   See 22 LA 608, 25 LA 118, 2 LA 870, 24 LA 33.

261.   See 30 LA 678, 27 LA 57, 29 LA 609, 27 LA 233, 28 LA 461.

262.   See 27 LA 174, 19 LA 815, 23 LA 171.

263.   See 27 LA 233.

264.   See 26 LA 438, 27 LA 57, 25 LA 281, 21 LA 330.

265.   See 24 LA 821, 26 LA 432, 24 LA 121, 26 LA 723, 19 LA 219.

266.   See 29 LA 609, 21 LA 330, 27 LA 671.

267.   See 26 LA 723, 22 LA 124, 27 LA 413.

268.   For a full treatment of this subject see Baer, Walter E., article in *Labor Law Journal,* October 1966.

269.   See 28 LA 330.

270.   See 23 LA 252.

271.   See 25 LA 736.

272.   See 43 LA 1262.

273. Neid v. Tassies Bakery, 219 Minn. 272, 17 N.W. 2d 357 (1945) (dicta that discharge is any permanent termination of employment); Stitt v. Locomotive Engineers Mutual Protective Association, 177 Mich. 207 (1913); in re: Public Ledger, 20 LRRM 2012. A typical definition is found in Adams v. Jersey Central Power & Light Co., 36 LRRM 2396.

274. See 28 LA 637.

275. See 17 LA 256.

276. See 17 LA 808.

277. See 47 LA 899, 1 LA 485, 9 LA 625, 18 LA 184, 24 LA 522, 40 LA 1343, 45 LA 97, 46 LA 297, 46 LA 583, 11 LA 598, 15 LA 702, 11 LA 345, 41 LA 386.

278. See 27 LA 321, 28 LA 121, 24 LA 761.

279. See 17 LA 227, 7 LA 583.

280. See 24 LA 95.

281. See 29 LA 23.

282. See 25 LA 663, 25 LA 774, 14 LA 986, 24 LA 421.

283. See 18 LA 919, 13 LA 294, 6 LA 617.

284. For a thorough study in this area see Phelps, Orme W. *Discipline and Discharge in the Unionized Firm.* Berkeley, Calif.: University of California Press, 1959.

285. See 25 LA 295, 25 LA 300, 24 LA 453.

286. See 45 LA 515, 42 LA 555.

287. For examples see 24 LA 630, 22 LA 756.

288. See 39 LA 352, 29 LA 272, 24 LA 804.

289. For full coverage of the subject of subsection (6) here, see Baer, Walter E. *Discipline and Discharge Under the Labor Agreement.* New York: American Management Association, 1972.

Index

A

Aaron, Benjamin, 141, 154
Abbreviations, 171
Abernathy, Byron, 69
Altieri, James V., 51, 68, 145
Aluminum Workers International Union, bargaining record, significance of, 135–36
American Arbitration Association (AAA), 138
   arbitrators supplied by, 13–16, 28–29, 37, 142–43
   counsel, representation by, rules governing, 153
   evidence, rules of, 141
American Bakeries Company, promptness of filing grievance, 82
American Body and Equipment Company, discipline of supervisor as grievance, 67
American Jurisprudence, 123
American Labor Arbitration Awards (ALAA), 42
American Pipe and Construction Company, grievance procedure time limits, 80
Anaconda Aluminum Company, bargaining record, significance of, 135–36
ARBIT, 9–11
Arbitrability, 50–61, 99–116; *see also specific issues in index*

Arbitrability—*Cont.*
   court proceedings for determination of, 99–102
   criteria for determination of, 101–2
   critical issues, 160–68; *see also specific issues in index*
   failure to comply with procedure, 104
   hearings, 113–15
   issues within or without scope of, 107–11
   merits versus threshold issue, 111–16
   precedent conditions, 103–7
   procedural issues, 103–7
   substantive issues, 107–11
   sufficiency of grievance, 105–6
   threshold issue of, 111–16
Arbitration
   ad hoc procedures, 22–28, 131
   alternatives to, 6
   complaints about process of, 94–95
   court proceedings versus, 86–87; *see also* Court proceedings
   criticisms, 3–5
   definitions, 1–6
   evidence, rules of, 138–51
   functions, 2, 169
   growing scope of, 18–21
   history, 6–7
   issues within or without scope of, 50–61, 99–116; *see also specific issues in index*

185